Live Love:

Master Vision And Vibration
To Create A Better World

Michelle Marie Angel

BALBOA.PRESS
A DIVISION OF HAY HOUSE

Balboa Press books may be ordered through booksellers or by contacting:

Balboa Press
A Division of Hay House
1663 Liberty Drive
Bloomington, IN 47403
www.balboapress.com
844-682-1282

Because of the dynamic nature of the Internet, any web addresses or links contained in this book may have changed since publication and may no longer be valid. The views expressed in this work are solely those of the author and do not necessarily reflect the views of the publisher, and the publisher hereby disclaims any responsibility for them.

The author of this book does not dispense medical advice or prescribe the use of any technique as a form of treatment for physical, emotional, or medical problems without the advice of a physician, either directly or indirectly. The intent of the author is only to offer information of a general nature to help you in your quest for emotional and spiritual well-being. In the event you use any of the information in this book for yourself, which is your constitutional right, the author and the publisher assume no responsibility for your actions.

Any people depicted in stock imagery provided by Getty Images are models, and such images are being used for illustrative purposes only. Certain stock imagery © Getty Images.

Print information available on the last page.

ISBN: 979-8-7652-2604-9 (sc)
ISBN: 979-8-7652-2606-3 (hc)
ISBN: 979-8-7652-2605-6 (e)

Library of Congress Control Number: 2022904587

Balboa Press rev. date: 05/25/2022

Contents

Dedication

To my Mother,
Bonnie Lou Yager

With deep love and gratitude
I dedicate this book to the soul
Who, as my mother, set an example
For excellence and integrity
And has always been a
Great Light in my Life

God Bless My Mother
Forever and Ever

Foreword

I always thought that this might be my favorite book ever. My inspiration for this book began back around 2001-2002 when I was living in California. I had written the outline and quite a bit of the content. I even submitted a manuscript to a publisher. But its time had not yet come.

My soul has ripened through these interim years, and I became more able to grasp and express the ideas that were meant to become the complete essence of the message of *Live Love*. I've written many other books called "Stories for Awakened Awareness" during this time span. All of my words express my own process of spiritual awakening and development. I've been exploring and creating a path through my transformational process. It has always been my intention to help others with personal transformation of consciousness. If I can find a way, I mused, then I can create a path of enlightenment for others to follow. Of course, I had my own higher beings that God send to me to follow.

My instructions and guidance has always come from within. Ultimately, my best method has been to commune with God in prayer and meditation, and to surrender to His Will. My morning time has always held a reservation for a time with God. I'm an avid seeker of truth and wisdom, and I have found the treasures in the kingdom of the soul.

No matter what happens in the outer world, I'm established in consciousness, with Heaven within. This has created equilibrium in my life. I've had plenty of challenges and stress, but it can never take hold of me. Like others on this path of ascension, I know what tools and processes to use to re-establish the center of peace.

It is my hope and prayer that the messages that I share through this book helps, feeds, nurtures, inspires, comforts, encourages, enlightens, and empowers all of you who read or listen to the words and feel the vibration of energy that is transmitted.

Much of it will serve to sanction and confirm your own personal growth process. All of us have much to share. All of us are here for a reason at this time in human history.

Let *Live Love* bring light into the world as we all master our creations through inspired visions and the pure love of God.

Acknowledgements

I thank God for being my Source of life and inspiration. If I hadn't grasped the concept and the deep inner sense of unconditional love, I would not have been able to overcome all of my challenges in life, let alone face God knowing my own impurities and mistakes. I'm so grateful to know the love of God. I know that through Jesus I am forgiven, and have learned to forgive, by following His example. My direct connection and relationship with God is the foundation of my life. I've been guided and protected and I am peaceful, happy, and grateful because of God, my rock.

I'm grateful for Universal Awareness and the realization of Oneness that encompasses every one of God's children. I love and appreciate the feeling of unity for and with all people. Any sense of division is dissolved in God's ubiquitous love. It is the viewpoint of my soul. It is true and it is real.

My inner life is complimented by all of the souls in my outer life on the earth plane. With that, I'd like to name a few.

Everyone who has ever played a role in my life has helped me to evolve. I acknowledge each and every one, and they each know who they are.

For the production of this book, I would like to offer a special thanks to Gary Fowler who has continuously and generously helped me along the way. A better friend one could never have. Truly, an angel.

A big thank you to Ann Minoza at Balboa Press and all of the production team who worked with me to get this book published and prepared to offer to the public.

I'd like to express a big heap of appreciation to Shane Pickering for swooping in at the last minute and solving some cover image design details. Miracles of God always show up in these timely sparkly moments.

There are blessings yet to come through angels showing up in my life. I'd like to send love and gratitude in advance for those I cannot yet name.

I'm transmitting love and blessings to every one of those of you reading this book. I've prayed a lot about blessing people through my writing, and God always answers my prayers. I hope you feel God's love pouring through the pages.

And, finally, I would like to acknowledge and express deep appreciation to all of my friends and family who are active in my life right now for loving and supporting me. You know who you are, so close your eyes, take a deep breath, and feel my love.

Love and Hugs to All,

Michelle Marie Angel

Introduction

It all starts with freedom. We are living, breathing soul entities shining light from our innermost beings. Freedom comes from the kingdom of the soul. The center of our energy field is eternal light. It is our connection with God, our Father, Creator of All—Great Spirit. With a deep connection to this center of our essential selves, we are boundless and limitless. We are all-knowing, all-seeing, and in control of our own destiny. We are the essence and power of Love, and love is all-powerful light as expressed by our radiance.

In order to become master of destiny, we must first know our True Self and our inherent powers. We are born sovereign and free. It is our right and our duty to remain sovereign and free. Our claim to freedom is marked by how we perceive ourselves, what we maintain of our own sovereignty, and how we manage our mind and heart. Our soul essence is infinite intelligence. It is the embodiment of Truth and reigns through our self-disciplined heart and mind. Self-control comes from our soul.

This book is about understanding self-mastery by wielding our natural abilities and powers. Our powers are much more vast than most of us have been led to believe. God gave us the freedom to wield our powers.

The first step is to assess our operating system within. The operating system is based on the source and frequency of information we hold in our subconscious mind. There are two types of operating systems, one is based on inner knowing of truth, and the other is based on programmed beliefs. One of the main themes in this book is about attunement to truth.

Some individuals have given over their minds to the television-based hive mind. Believing this form of information intake to be benign, they have inadvertently been programmed by vision and vibration which was not sourced from within. When individuals are strong in their inner faith, the programming has less of an effect. The degree of influence to the subconscious mind varies based on how much one has maintained sovereignty of mind, heart, and soul. The development of conscience is essential for personal mastery.

No matter how sovereign a person is, the subtle manipulation of perception may have its effects. The most masterful souls spend more time with people and nature than technology. And even more important than being with other living souls, is to spend some time in quiet solitude. It is essential to get away from any sort of group mind or group think on a regular basis to generate the expression of the essential self.

Live Love is designed to help recalibrate your consciousness. It is a path to coming home. There is deep peace that is felt in the depths of the soul. It is a reprieve from outer activities and its treasures are unlimited. With a secure connection to God, the innermost source of being, we can reflect our own divinity and perfection. We can catch and comprehend the meaning, purpose, peace, ethics, morals, values, and gifts of our lives. We will be empowered by our personal genius within, our essential True Self, and express our highest potential without interference, and in harmonious cooperation with our Glorious God and all the universe.

All the resources of the world come from Source. We are partners with God when we attune to the highest vibration of Spirit and the highest vision locked within the seed of our soul. All we have to do is look at this inner map and find the treasures.

This book is God's gift to the souls who wish to validate the treasures that are personal and unique to each reader or listener. All is already known within, but with the confirmation of what you already know, you will have the strength, courage, and love to move forward in your life with confidence, inspiration, and passion.

There are no accidents. If this book has come into your life, then it is time for you to receive God's perfect love and blessings that are made just for you. Enjoy your journey as you reclaim the keys to your inner kingdom and reclaim your soul's true perfection. You are loved.

God Bless you as you read this book, during every step of your life's journey, and as you receive every breath of life forever and ever.

Michelle Marie Angel

Chapter Thirteen

THE END IS THE BEGINNING
CREATING DESTINATION AND FOCUS

> *By creating a vision of the end result,
> we choose our destination, our future.*

Our life as we knew it is has ended. We are now re-creating our lives and our world with the power of love. With vision and hope for our future, we can march boldly ahead in our lives with joy and enthusiasm. We know our True Selves. We know the power of love. We hold steadfast to our vision of Heaven on Earth. We are conscious creators. This is only the beginning.

New Beginnings

The beginning of any endeavor is to envision the end. I'm speaking to each of you reading or listening to this message. I know there are no accidents in life and that *you* are meant to hear this message now. I invite you, my dear reader, to take a journey into a vision of our best hoped for future. I invite you to increase your sense of personal power and claim your Divine birthright of peace and freedom.

As a global society, we notice things that are happening in the world that are not desirable or acceptable. Many people are suffering. Mis-creations and agendas are threatening to lead to annihilation.

But that is merely the perfect catalyst for change! It's time to wake up and change directions. Our true destiny is at hand.

With a greater understanding of the nature of life, and the power of our consciousness and how to wield our true power, we can control what we experience. As we realize we are creating our life and world through our thoughts and feelings, we are waking up to a new paradigm of reality. We used to think that "what we see is what we get" but we now realize that "what we get is what we see." That's vision!

We must create a vision of the future we desire and give it plenty of our attention. We can realize our true inner power and become masters of our own minds—conscious, subconscious, and superconscious. We are doing that by coming to know our True Whole Self.

Shift *is* Happening

Personally, we are each feeling a shift that is changing our lives and world and it seems really chaotic. Don't you feel different now? We're all feeling it. We notice that changes in our lives are occurring more rapidly. Our relationships, health, our jobs, and our self-assuredness are all caught up in the earth's energy wobble. We are shifting internally and externally. Some days we feel great and the next day we feel like shift!

Did you think it was just you? It's not! Somehow our attention is being summoned by these inner feelings and outer manifestations of change. God is calling our attention to attune to Divine love and flow with our natural evolution.

This is a shift in consciousness occurring, a transformational paradigm shift, that is affecting our world. Our level of awareness is increasing, individually and globally that is causing us to change. This change is a fundamental change that affects the way we think, what we say, what we do, how we feel, our inner senses, and how we relate to others. It affects our relationship with life: our world, our nation, our community, our religious and educational institutions, our family members, our friends, our jobs, our finances, our health, our environment, and our very Self.

We are now aware of what it means to carry a high vibration. We are more acutely aware of the power of our thoughts and feelings. We know we can control our vibration. We are learning to gain and maintain inner peace. This is a journey. This is a major transformation. We are free in our minds. We can change everything that seems amiss to something better. We can move toward perfection in body, mind, heart, and soul.

It's a movement. It's an inner inspired inclination that is pushing us forward to provide solutions and positive change. It's an influx of light that is revealing the truth. All sorts of things are coming up for healing. Our whole society is waking up. The global community is standing up for truth and what is right.

We have seen abuse of power. We have seen hoarding of resources. We have uncovered agendas and people who say one thing and do another. We are Truth Warriors standing up to individuals and organizations that do not serve the greater good. The truth is being revealed and it is accelerating in its power to create change for the better.

There's no going back. Although this shift is causing a profound impact on our lives, there's no way we can go back to our old ways. It just doesn't work any longer.

There is a new paradigm of living that is emerging. Understanding how life works in the new paradigm is crucial. My desire is to inspire hope and faith by conveying an understanding of essential truth that can be lived. These truths can be easily understood and applied by everyone with some simple living processes and practices.

The fundamental truth that "life is energy" is foundational. A full understanding of this allows us to realize our personal power and to use it most efficiently and effectively. We *are* energy and we are the directors!

All energy carries information. Consciousness is Light, is Truth, and is information. We have to know that we have the ability to receive the Light of Truth, to walk in the Light of Truth by staying in integrity, and by becoming the Light of Truth by embodying the highest vibrational wisdom that is born of Love's intelligence. In other words, we are living into a new paradigm through expanded heart intelligence that is pure Spirit in expression. We are conscious that we are consciousness which has the inherent ability to translate energy from one form of light to another form of light. This involves "comprehending the light" and mastering the energy. Learning about our personal energy field, how to obtain light from our Source, and how to live life according to our soul's purpose is becoming the new norm.

Our Source of energy is God. We spend our life energy by directing our attention. We are creating in every moment, so it's imperative we focus on only what we choose to create. If we can consciously turn our attention away from worry, fear, problems, hate, greed, jealousy, anger, and lack, we can experience a joyful abundant life. Everyone can.

Anybody who wants to help this world has the power to do so. We can help first by consciously raising our awareness and helping others to raise their awareness. This is the resurrection: from the denser vibrations of the physical to the lighter vibrations of spirit or pure consciousness. The inner shift of attention to our causal consciousness of outer form empowers us to shift from victims of the physical realm to masters of the physical realm. We are transcending material challenges with a spiritual perspective of our essential nature of light intelligence. We are naturally sovereign and free.

*Personal power has been downgraded by the belief that governments have the balance of power to affect the outcome of our earthly existence. This is **not** the case. In fact, that is part of the shift: moving away from outer governance to governance from within.*

We each have power individually that makes a big difference.

Our power lies in knowing our sovereignty within. Our perceptual inner resources are based in our inherent inner knowing. Our eternal essential Self is always glowing. We are light. By placing our attention on our inner light within and following that light with our mind and body, our inner light grows stronger and stronger. Our deepest intelligence is strong and certain. We are powerful. Although unseen by the physical sight, our inner light is a power that affects others tremendously. We have much more power that we are aware of. We have much more of an effect on our world around us that we realize. The light that we are is Spirit, and we keep getting more luminous as we develop our inner strength.

Humanity is united in Spirit. As we each raise our level of vibration individually, we compensate those of lower vibration as the wholeness of Spirit equalizes. In that way, we help to raise the overall vibration of the collective consciousness. The higher we raise and maintain our vibration, the more we help other individual souls to increase their level of vibration. In addition, when we set specific intentions for making the world a better place, our energy combines with others of the same intentions. Those intentions are powered by our will and create fields of energy that gain in power to further affect the consciousness of others. Shared intentions also create magnetic fields. People with similar intentions attract one another and synchronistic experiences happen. Not only is it clear that changing yourself changes the world, but also new alliances of cooperation are formed, and the world just keeps getting better. We are each powerful agents of change.

Group Consciousness

There are many like-minded conscious people forming groups to herald in our new world of peace and harmony. This focused group energy has powerful effects. More of us can begin to use it in our own small groups as well as networking with larger groups.

The undercurrents of peaceful intentions and loving cooperative energy by the masses that are uniting are being felt throughout the world—even the politicians know it. The major political powers that wish to control or destroy are now feeling impotent against this energy. The old ways, fueled by power and control energy, are just not working any longer. They are based on greed, deception, and other forms of illusion. That energy may take a little more time to completely dissipate, but it *is* leaving our planet. That dissolution is accelerating right now. We need to remember to not dwell on it too much. We must be aware enough to put an end to it by declaring and decreeing with our spoken word that it MUST GO! But we can also realize that its existence IS waning. That vibration is being transmuted by the awakening masses.

You can help by not giving it your attention (your energy) to promote its existence. With more attention to love than fear, they lose their power. Negative energy toward any individual or situation does not help! Placing your attention on each person's good aspects will illuminate them and help them grow out of their old ways.

We simply withdraw all the power from the old guard by not following along with the old programs or naughty agendas. The bad actors are all being exposed. Their true intentions based on greed and control are evident and they cannot be taken seriously. Laugh at their plans! Everything is being exposed. Some laws have been made that are corrupt. Doing the right thing is sometimes a matter of civil disobedience. They go against the principles of God which is peace, freedom, and goodwill toward all.

There are some politicians who are in alignment with this positive peace-loving energy. Their numbers are growing. Watch for them and give them full support.

There are also independent researchers and journalists who are supplying information to reveal corruption so that we can put an end to it. We've been inculcated, programmed, and brainwashed to think there is lack in the world. Not true. We have the intelligence and infinite Source within to resolve all energy into its perfection.

We will not fall prey to transhumanist agendas or become enslaved in any way. We will not be deceived by corporate interests that corrupt our institutions, our health, and our way of life. Love is the ultimate power. Love is winning!

You Are Making a Difference

It's time to stop in our tracks and really tune in to what's happening. I'm here to tell you right now, reader, that you already *are* making a difference. When you change the energy inside of yourself by creating inner peace, you are making a hugely beneficial energetic contribution to our world. By controlling your reactions to people to create peace while relating, you are really making an enormous difference. Keep up the good work!

With the understanding that I am conveying in this book, I believe that you will continue to shift how you think about Life and regain a greater sense of personal power. You will greatly influence the direction we are going to choose next—as an individual and as part of our global society.

There is a paradox here. At the same time we gain personal power to influence the direction of our society, we surrender to the power that has been creating and maintaining life all along. There is a Divine plan being carried out here. We just need to surrender personal control and get in tune with what that Divine plan is and what our individual part is. With this attunement we can work in peaceful cooperation to create something new and better.

When we are aligned with Divine intention individually, we are all tapped into the same source. This provides a foundation of unity from which to create a better world. We can navigate in Life by listening to our hearts and flowing with the spirit of love. By listening to our hearts, we harmonize with all by getting in tune with our inherent Divinity. We get information about our individual part. The things we are most passionate about lead us to our personal work. Inner work comes before outer work. It takes some adjustment to get in tune and stay attuned within. There is a power from centering our attention within, toward our core, toward our Source of infinite information. Our true field of consciousness is nonlocal and nonlinear. We are free of any limitations of time or space or outer circumstances. More on that later in Chapter 5.

We are moving into experiences that bring greater and greater joy during these evolutionary times. We can easily create peace while learning to express from the essence of our souls. And we hold the space for others to ascend in their own time as well.

The strength in unity that we create with unified intentions is changing the world. There are several tips that I'm going to share in this book that will make you say "Ah-Ha! Mmmmm... That makes sense; it rings true. It seems so simple, why didn't I think of that?" Or maybe you already had that one, but another tip is new to you. Sometimes it was just a fleeting thought and it just needs more attention. Or maybe you are just at the place where you needed confirmation or validation. We are all at different stages and there's a huge scope of changes taking place. Maybe somehow you got distracted and didn't focus on this new way of being yet. Well, this book is about focus. Let the journey begin...

Destiny

What is your destiny? What is the destiny of our world? It's all about choice. It's up to you to choose yours. It's up to the whole of humanity to choose our planet's destiny, but you are on that team with the rest of us.

We need you! We need you to become acutely aware of your personal power to impact the circumstances of our earthly existence. We need you to use your talents and gifts and support humanity in our major transformation. Each time you help one, you help all.

Nobody needs to fall prey to fear. Nobody needs to feel like they are being victimized by life or world conditions. It's time for empowerment. Get inspiration and follow your intuition. Then follow your map provided by synchronicities. Always remember to ask questions within and expect answers to come. They will!

> *If we perceive ourselves as victims, we will be.*
> *If we realize our creative powers within*
> *and use them cooperatively,*
> *we can create the kind of life and world that we truly desire.*

By understanding the energy system of life, and by adopting a creator perspective, we can change the world. We will make our personal lives happy and fulfilling as well.

People are already using their creative powers, but most of us don't realize how. We don't fully see the cause and effect connection between our thoughts and feelings and the reality of our lives, let alone the world. We have been using our creative powers unconsciously. By becoming aware of how we acquire and direct our energy we can create our individual and group experiences consciously. Doesn't that sound better than waiting around to "see" what is going to happen?

It *is* all about seeing. Our visions can be perception (outside in; or inspired from within) or projection (inside out). We use perception to sense our current outer reality, or to delve deep into consciousness. We use projection when we vision something that we intend (or fear) to happen in the future. By fully realizing how we are creating our outer reality within our inner world of thought and feeling, we can choose to have a peaceful paradise on earth where all is well for all life on this planet. We can each create our own lives where we enjoy love and abundance fully. We start by directing our attention consciously. We monitor our thoughts and feelings to be in alignment with our intentions. We use mental imaging. We learn how to raise our vibration, or emotional energy, and to transmute energy that is lower in nature. Our heart is a source of radiation. We can amplify and direct that radiation by our thoughts and control of emotion. We can use our feelings as a source of information. We can employ our imagination to meet our soul's inspiration. Our intuitive information will guide us to create the highest and best for ourselves and our world.

It is all energy. Your personal energy counts. You can direct it toward creating a joyful existence in a peaceful paradise as long as you focus your attention on that intention. By the end of this book, you will realize more of your own personal power and how to create consciously. Your life will improve dramatically and rapidly for the better. So will our world as a result of your attention shift. Enjoy! (By the way, we ALL love you!)

Creating our Destiny

Our destiny is what we make it. By increasing our awareness of life and turning our attention to our soul essence, our resulting empowerment will make a positive destiny not only possible, but it will turn probability to actuality.

By connecting to our soul, we are connected to the whole, consciously. We become aware of our Life Purpose, follow our hearts, and tune in to the changes that are happening in our world. When we become clear about what we desire, then we can create exactly that.

It all starts by mastering our minds where we are inherently free.

> *Imagination is the key to destination.*

Imagination is not idle daydreaming. It is our fundamental ability to create. Things are not always as they seem, but an inquisitive heart and mind can always find the way to the solution for challenging situations. In other words, things may look one way while looking from one point of view, but by shifting perspectives, it takes on a whole new appearance. And then, by deep introspection in the stillness of the soul, clear intelligence presents Itself.

I'm going to share some ideas that will help shift your perspective and increase your perceptions. With a new way to look at life, and by focusing attention/energy on solutions, our future will become one of hope and excitement for wonderful times to come.

> *By focusing your attention on positive solutions*
> *with a feeling of love, you can make*
> *extremely rapid beneficial changes.*

Get Solution-Focused

We direct energy with our attention. If we corral our energies from all the distractions and programming that is capturing our attention, we can use this energy to focus on solutions. The solutions are unfolding right now. Just tune in.

When we really learn to focus our attention in every moment—and this takes practice—we can really make some quick beneficial changes. I'm going to make some suggestions on how to obtain and focus on solutions both for individuals and for cooperating groups. Then we can synergize our consciousness with others and focus on solutions with unified intent and *really* use our power!

By developing your customized version of "Bulls-Eye Faith" on which to focus your attention, you will automatically attract into your life that which you consciously choose to create. You will have a rich personal belief system based on inner truth and be able to envision personal and global solutions. (*Bulls-Eye Faith* is the companion "Inner Work" book that goes along with *Live Love*.)

You will be able to use your own energy much more efficiently. You will have a strong sense of purpose. You will create alignment in many areas: mind-body-soul, conscious-subconscious-super conscious, thoughts-words-actions, and intuitive truth-thoughts-expectations.

You can develop a powerful laser-like focus of your personal energy and manifest your own dreams. You will positively improve the experiences of your life as you help make the world a better place. You will be using the principles of quantum physics to get the most efficient use of your personal energy.

You will have a deep inner sense of personal power. With your newly realized power you can use your unique talents and abilities to create what your soul desires, thus bringing about a total sense of personal fulfillment. You will definitely notice a sense of renewal and a surge of inner joy by being solution-focused. Joy ensues naturally as you express creativity from your Eternal essence of Being.

You may be drawn to cooperate with others in a synergistic unified focus toward solutions. Whatever your life purpose is, it will become clear to you by looking within.

The world needs you! Are you ready?

The Vision

Here's what I envision with love as the result of all of us waking up to love: I see an increased understanding of life. I see a renewed and powerful sense of hope. I see an absolute resolution and application of faith. I see and feel you and I and our fellow humans in tune with the spirit of love. I see people being kind always. I see each of us feeling like a powerful creator—never a victim. I see everyone being inspired to find their personal life purpose and using their unique gifts. I see us each consciously transforming ourselves and sharing our experiences to help others. I see people transforming negative energies in their personal space back into the energy of love. I see high vibrations in individual energy fields and in the co-joined collective energy field. I see fields of consciousness focused on singular intentions that are powerful agents of innovation and positive change.

I see and feel energy being used constructively toward life. I see and feel the underlying love and our renewed spiritual connection causing people to have goodwill toward all. I see and feel each person spending their time and energy doing exactly what they enjoy doing— nothing more and nothing less. I see everyone experiencing perfect health and abundance.

I see and feel a deepening sense of personal freedom. I see all of us feeling and expressing the unique version of love that we are as our primary life experience. I see and sense a whole world of sharing and caring. I see the whole planet being completely cleaned up and living harmoniously—it feels refreshing! I see an awareness of Oneness, of unity, spreading across all humanity. I see the beauty of life expanding.

We can have it all. First, we start at knowing where we want to end up. We just go there in the now moment, because the future is simply now expanded by vision. We place our attention on these positive thoughts and feelings and help the seeds of their potential existence to grow. Our hope becomes belief. We build our faith around it. Then we discover and use our personal tools and awareness that will craft our next life experience and world conditions.

We really *do* have the ability to create the kind of life and world we desire. We *can* create a vision of peace on our planet *and* have that experience right now in this moment. Go team!

It's All About Choice

Each individual has one choice to make: will you serve money and old ways of being, or will you serve love and new ways of being? We no longer live in a world confined to a materialistic definition of self and reality. We know that life emerges from Spirit—the Light of consciousness. The greater Self is united by love. This book is for those who choose to serve love. It is for those who are open to new understandings that create a magnificent outlook for our bright co-created future.

Notice how many of us have quit our jobs because we realized our integrity was at stake. And even though it gave us financial security, we HAD to do the right thing. Our conscience rules. Sometimes it's hard to find the courage and means to make the switch. But it is literally becoming a matter of life or death. We have courage. We have faith. We have what it takes to overcome and still thrive in the face of the possible repercussions financially.

This is an opportunity to step up to the plate. It's time to look deep within and find our inner passion. Indeed, that passion is being inspired and stoked with an imminent need for change.

This is the time when creative energy inspires us to follow our dreams. More and more of us are doing what we love. This is the time. We are supporting each other. We are fully supported by the new energy in our world.

Faith in ourselves is foundational. We are backed by all. Our True Whole Self is our place of power. We center! We buck up and remain in the eye of the storm by staying in the center of our holistic power where we are one with God, our Almighty Father. We are never abandoned. We are never alone. We are humbled and we are empowered all at once through the grace and wisdom of Almighty God. Amen to that.

The Power of Love

The power of love has been noted in the past, but right now it's really time to take heed and use love to our full advantage. Our fundamental essence IS love; it is the Source of all Life. We have an unlimited Source of love to enjoy and use. It is a magnet that we can use to attract what we want in our lives. We can pour its energy into images of what we *consciously choose* to have exist in our lives and on our planet. Love's source is from our unified whole and creates unity and abundance for all. It is infinite and all-inclusive. It is the highest intelligence. All we have to do is understand how to express and use love's intelligent magnetism and marry it to our inspired imagination.

> **With a focus on love and our intentional creations, everything else will dissipate as energy is transformed.**

Our future is now. We are actually stepping into the present more fully and grasping the impact of our individual power by using presence consciousness.

We used to think of money as our tool to create what we wanted. I'm going to demonstrate how applications of love and imagination create shortcuts to manifesting personal and world solutions and abundance in every form.

The two key ingredients to creating the life and world that we choose are love and attention. We focus our attention on images, or forms, whether in our outer world or our thoughts and images in our inner world. We are about to embark on an exciting adventure to direct our attention solely, with pure focus, on the peaceful world that is our unified intention. Combined with the energy of pure love our success is guaranteed.

Has manipulation or fear attracted your attention? Anything that you give your attention to you are giving your energy to and are helping to create. Are you really sure that *everything* you think about is what you want to create? When you continually ask yourself this question, your thought processes and feelings begin to change. It is a process, so be patient with yourself. Allow processes to complete their purpose.

When you can at once be present with your outer reality through your senses *and* draw your attention away from your current life circumstances, you can change your life by placing your attention within on new thoughts and feelings, consciously chosen.

Drama, Distraction, Derailment

You may have realized by now that there are some people who are not deriving energy from their Source within. They create drama. They usurp your attention. Some are conscious energy thieves, some are not. Most probably just haven't learned yet about energy, its Source and their direct connection, and how to be sovereign. But you can set boundaries and lovingly put a stop to their antics. It is a service to them to put a stop to it.

Distractions are things that draw your attention that are not productive or conducive to maintaining a high vibration. We've been geared toward giving our attention and power away to television, print media, social media, and "experts" that really are not. As we consciously shift our attention, we become aware of these things and increase our discernment. Again, this is a process of transformation, and it takes time to make a permanent shift.

Going down a wrong path can cause a derailment to your focus on your life purpose or inspired beneficial goals. Anything that takes you off your path that focuses your attention on your personal mission and ascension goals, is a derailment. Recognize it, then just get back on track. If, however, it is an unavoidable challenge, use it for personal growth. It might be part of your soul's plan. You can discern within the stillness of your soul how to navigate through circumstances and ordeals. Just stay connected to Source within and the hindrance will be transformed into wisdom.

There are a lot of tricks, traps, and obstacles along the way. Each one provides an opportunity to hone your skills of focused attention. Each time we make adjustments, we live a more conscious lifestyle.

Consciously Choose Attention Focus

If we are conscious of where we focus our attention, and if we use love as our tool and navigation device, we can steer our individual lives and the whole world directly toward solutions that create an abundance of love, joy, and peace. We can maintain our God given freedom. We can each use our creative energy freely, do *only* what we truly love to do, and have fun in the process of Life. We *can* and *will* live together in peace. Let's turn up the love! Ready? Let's do it!

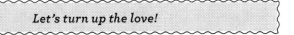

Let's turn up the love!

Let's Create!

By creating a vision of the end result, we choose our destination, our future.

It becomes the place where we consciously direct our energies. As we live more consciously, we can live on purpose with our visions in mind. We can set our goals and intentions around the vision of our destination. We can learn to focus our energies entirely on that vision. As we inject our visions with the power of love, we set the energy in motion to create the manifestation of a life and world that we truly desire. We need to apply some concentration. Although seemingly magic at first, this is science and results are certain.

We are heading toward peace, regardless of any contrary evidence. The movement toward a world that operates with the energy of peaceful cooperation is picking up momentum. Will you help?

Let's Imagine...

Just pretend that all of humanity has already begun to love one another and cooperate. What would life be like? What if we realized that everything that happens in Life has a purpose and we just accept it and stop creating inner havoc by our resistance? What if by creating this constant inner peace, we affect others to be peaceful as well?

Imagine people sharing love in a variety of ways. Total acceptance. Kindness. Understanding. Forgiveness. Lots of hugs and kisses! Smiles. Sharing our unique expressions of creativity. Sharing everything we have. Helping. Let's imagine everyone acting out of consideration for others, having good will toward all. This is Divine love. It's about caring and sharing. It comes from Spirit and it is pure.

Imagine the environment as completely clean and pristine. Imagine clean air, water, and land. Imagine unlimited sources of energy that are readily available for all of our purposes. Imagine living a holistic lifestyle in cooperative communities and networked groups from all around the globe. Imagine the sense of security that is felt by all.

Imagine everybody experiencing perfect health and vitality. Imagine all internal energy systems flowing freely and living harmoniously with the fruits of the planet.

Imagine everyone being truthful with themselves and others. Imagine how it feels to be able to express in total freedom without judgment or repercussion. Imagine the expression of individual authenticity highlighting the uniqueness of each person.

Imagine personal impeccability rising to the level where there was total transparency—everybody knowing the truth about everyone else. Imagine all acts of greed and secrecy being exposed by the masses who know the truth through inner intuition and outer confirmation.

Imagine feeling the joy of doing only what our hearts desire; of serving others and creating from our essence. Imagine all of the homemade gifts that people are making because they can spend all of their time on what used to be their hobbies to create material abundance in their lives. What joy and delight we feel both as givers and receivers!

Let's imagine people actively implementing solutions to world hunger. Imagine each and every person experiencing all forms of abundance. Imagine everyone feeling the sense that there is plenty for all and the essence of sharing is prevalent among all people. Food and clean water is abundant and distributed to all; shared with all. All are full and happy!

Imagine the ease of living.

Imagine that genuine spirit of love that we all have inside of us being expressed to the fullest. Imagine all people living in total freedom governed only by the power of love from their hearts. Truth and integrity reign!

This is not a pipe dream! This can be realized now with the knowledge and application of our innate powers. We can join forces in consciousness and heal humanity and our planet with the alchemy of love. Let's learn how to make a better reality together and do it now.

Now is our time. Our time is now. Now holds infinite potential of our united vision.

Chapter One

LIFE ON EARTH
Awareness and Personal Power

> *We learn many things in life,*
> *but what we really need to learn about is Life itself.*

The Alchemy of Consciousness

Catalysts of human evolution may seem daunting at times, but in the end our consciousness is transformed permanently to higher states of being. The benefits far, far surpass the heart and soul refinement processes of overcoming human challenges.

While at first, the challenges may seem overwhelming, information arrives from the genius creativity from our True Self within that saves the day.

At the onset of sudden, seemingly insurmountable, circumstances in our lives and in our world we are shocked. We have just entered a "Jonathon Livingston Seagull" event. I take that term from the book title that describes a sudden, radical paradigm shift. One reality that is being experienced that seems the perpetual norm suddenly shifts. Some cataclysm acts as a catalyst for change, then, unexpectedly and rapidly, a whole new reality presents itself. There is no way around it. It must be gone *through*.

Alchemy is change. Consciousness is the Light of Being. It is the whole eternal self that reckons with the false identities and illusions of lower natures. This reckoning transmutes all energies that are unlike its pure essential eternal nature. When the falsities are revealed, they dissolve.

Pure Spirit is the identity of our soul. It is infinite intelligence. The true self is Divine, undivided as One, and the vibration of pure love. Herein lies our power. Our freedom and sovereignty is at stake. Our true identity has the power to overcome all challenges being presented at this time.

All of humanity is being alchemized. Simultaneously in an interwoven fashion, we are individually and collectively being alchemized. There is tremendous inner and outer shift happening.

By now, I think we all realize at some place in the scope of awareness that change is afoot. Buckle up! Be prepared by understanding the meaning and purpose of these unprecedented changes. Only good will come of it.

Collective Human Consciousness: Death and Re-birth

The transformation of consciousness of the human collective is no less than profound, no less than radical, and yet it is marked by the Divine Hand of God. The power of Spirit is Absolute. Only victory is possible. Anything, no matter how dire, that is intended for evil, God—that Divine Spark within each of our souls—uses for good. Having faith in the perfect outcome, described as vision in the previous chapter, is the foundation for transformational success.

The old ways and institutions are dying. There is a great revival of souls turning to God. The direct connection to the Holy Spirit is becoming ever stronger through prayer and communion. The union through communion is the all-powerful force that can reckon with any outer condition or cataclysm. The power of the soul is activated to dominate the outer through the inner.

That being said, the very real processes of going through the feelings and mental impact of such radical changes is real. The shift includes the processes of going through great loss. There is shock. There is denial. There is mourning. These processes can't be denied or overlooked. Crying is a part of the transformation. It is an alchemical act of releasing and transforming energy. When done in conjunction with prayer and visioning, it is an extremely powerful tool as well.

Eventually, acceptance of the truth that has come to light, or the reality of the loss or cataclysm sets in. Now healing begins. The healing energy is compassion for self and others. There are personal tragedies, community disasters, as well as national and global adversities. Personal loss and self-compassion comes first. Heal yourself and gain strength and wisdom and become equipped to help others and serve the greater good. Ask for and receive divine guidance. Continue prayer and communion and observe the incoming help and blessings. Feel your strength grow.

Once healed and prepared for service, it's time to take inspired action to rebuild our health, communities, and environment. Each one of us has a specific purpose and it all begins with helping those who are right here around us. Expansion of service will be organic. It will happen naturally through pure intuition and inspiration.

Anything is possible. We increase the probability of positive outcomes through personal and collective mastery of consciousness. We wield our power through vision and vibration. We are equipped with strength, courage, and wisdom.

Human Evolution: Caterpillars to Butterflies

An inner reflection recorded during my
soul's transformational process:

As I observe the outer world and see the propensity for human death and destruction through deception and corruption, my heart grows heavy with concern. As usual, I took my concerns to God in my heart through communion.

I asked for resurrection. I was feeling low in spirit. I do not wish to witness the demise of family or friends, or anyone in my greater family—humanity.

Once again, I was comforted as I sought to see God's purposes revealed. I was reminded that life is Eternal. I know that. I know there is no death in my heart, but when I look out toward the experiences of people who have been deceived and have died from obvious medical tyranny…well, I just need answers.

I know for certain that everything works together for good and that God has a purpose for everything. My comfort comes from that knowledge and from the deeper communion where I can ask for further explanation. That's when I got God's answer: humans are being transformed from "caterpillars to butterflies."

In my heart, I was reminded about the transfiguration of Jesus. The time he was with two of his disciples and he had turned to a brilliant essence of light and also was visited by two people from heaven. He explained that the veil between the worlds was very thin. I think we pierce it all the time in certain states of consciousness.

My best friend growing up, Linda, passed to the other side at the age of forty-six. She had a terminal illness and we had conversations when she knew she was about to cross over. We both knew that life is eternal and that we would be living in different dimensions and that we could communicate. We established a code word three days before she passed. The code word is "mud." We had made "falling in the mud" a code in fifth grade for an incident that happened that we didn't want to speak about overtly. It came from that.

Yesterday, I was reading a story to a student where I work at an educational tutoring type center, and I turned a page to the next chapter and the first word in the title was "Mud." Of course, I knew Linda was with me. Then, last night I had a dream. In the dream, I was calling Linda who seemed to be taking college classes far away. I was asking her to come home and telling her that I missed her. I just remember the feeling of calling to her with my heart feeling very strong.

Today, I was reading a book at my home, and again, I ran across the word "mud."

You see, I had called to God this morning and asked for some understanding and some comfort. I was feeling distraught over the medical tyranny and worldwide political corruption situation. I knew that some of my close loved ones were not aware. At the same time, I had been gathering information about the injections through articles and videos revealing the ingredients and the medical implications of those ingredients.

Besides the principle of God's purpose that I always look to in order to see what good is going to come from things, I also know that the principle of focusing on solutions is important to create higher, better, and miraculously perfect outcomes.

What is the solution, God? Well, if we are transforming our consciousness to higher levels of being, then we ought to be able to heal as Jesus did. He did say: "Follow me." To me, that means follow his lead and do as he does. He teaches by example.

Two things seem to be the key in healing: vibration and vision. Jesus raised the vibration in his body to the highest pure love that matched God, the Father. Father God maintains the highest vibration and vision for us. When we become One with our Father in Heaven in the vibration of pure love, then we can also seek and download the highest vision of perfection. In the case of healing we hold the image of perfect health.

I'm just a student on this path. I'm in the process of learning and transforming my own consciousness. But I know, if I keep at it, I can learn and apply the scientific laws of the universe and adapt my consciousness the way Jesus did. By this means, I hope to reverse any adverse effects on people that may cause disease, suffering, and death. I know that others share this intention.

God raised me to be a teacher. I am also determined to be a healer.

I'm just writing these words as a process in real time. I know that there is an alchemy of consciousness occurring in myself and all others.

This is the greater purpose.

My friend, Linda, is reaching out to me from Heaven. She makes me feel as if we are working together in some way. I'll learn more as time goes on. Maybe the higher learning she is receiving is what she is getting from the other side, and maybe she is going to share it with me.

I know one thing—love never dies. And with that bond, we can be assured that life goes on and on and on. We just evolve to higher states of being and everything we are experiencing right now is serving God's purposes.

My vibration is set to pure love, compassion, and forgiveness. I observe my own changes in consciousness. My thoughts are changing. My responses are more loving. My heart feels more pure. I'm attempting to maintain my focus on the patterns of perfection, or images from the Divine Mind of God.

May all of humanity be comforted at this time of accelerated evolution. I hope that all hold tight to the knowledge that: "Everything works together for good for those who love God, for those who are called according to his purpose." Romans 8:28

Wake Up World!

It's time to stop playing "business as usual" and wake up to our own creative powers within. It's time to become aware of the global Self, and how we affect each other and the planet. We are really just now waking up to how we create our own lives!

We've already had several wake up calls. The many court trials, such as the O.J. Simpson debacle, has showed us that our justice system does not necessarily uphold justice and that our attention is up for grabs. The media tends to create distractions that holds our awareness hostage while avoiding the truth of more pertinent information. September 11 demonstrated that there are dark forces that can sneak up and catch us unaware while causing great destruction and an enormous loss of lives. Deceptive strategies of trusted persons in authoritative institutions will run us over unless we open our eyes and stand up for ourselves.

At the time of this writing, there has been an impeachment show, a covid scamdemic, election fraud, evidence of world-wide corruption based in banking, Satanism, and pedophilia, and all driven by corrupt people using a weaponized media that have influenced some minds to perceive one thing, while all the while they are hiding information that implicates them in heinous crimes and systemic corruption. There has been a drain on the common people of the world while banks, governments, and corporations have tried to control people and resources while causing great destruction on our planet.

Worst of all, our children have been the targets of maligned minds and dark cycles ruled by abuse of power. Lying, deception, and murder have sought to keep truth hidden. Our children have suffered abuse of power from many directions. Sexual abuse, ritual abuse, chemical abuse, mental and emotional abuse, and suppression of their inner light, natural rights, and neglect of their needs. Some parents are complicit, while others suffer from abuse of power when trying to do the right thing for their children.

Those globalists with eugenic principles at their roots have wreaked havoc. The use of euphemisms and outright lies, saying one thing while meaning another in policies, laws, and agendas have deceived the masses of humanity for quite some time.

There are many critical environmental issues. Many of these issues caused by weaponized technology. The extent of these issues is largely hidden from our awareness, but they have caused much destruction to many lives and our planet. The evidence of this destruction is dying species, lower longevity rates among humanity, and violated ecosystems. We are witnessing the increase in the all-cause mortality rates and the decrease of fertility. This has been all by design.

The first step in waking up is to become fully aware of what is going on. I don't mean watch the news on television, either. Much of the truth is missing when it comes to television news, and the truth that is presented is often twisted to create fear and sensationalism. It takes much discernment to sort out the truth from the propaganda narratives. There are tactics that have been consciously implemented to sway our belief system for an agenda that is not conducive to our own personal welfare. What I mean is to *really* find out what's going on from people and organizations that care. Not everybody can become an activist for every problem on earth, but by becoming aware and *focusing our attention on solutions*, each one of us can make a huge difference. In our hearts we each have concerns that are more emphasized for us that leads us to our passion. Our passion leads us to our purpose.

Solutions do not include pointing fingers and placing blame. But it does mean finding out the truth, holding those who act against humanity responsible and accountable, and making changes to benefit the welfare of the people and all life. First and foremost, participate in the changing of the guard. That means relieve those in positions of power of their duties and replace them when they are corrupt, immoral, unethical, or out of integrity. If they use their position of power for selfish gain, get rid of them. Abuse of power has to end.

Putting undue attention on the causes of the problems and the perpetrators does not foster solutions. Awareness of the situations and causes, for the purposes of finding resolution and positive change, is indeed, necessary.

It's time to stop inadvertently supporting unending wars that support the banksters and corrupt politicians with corporate interests. Get the power and powerful weaponry, including drugs, out of the hands of irresponsible people.

> *If the rug is pulled out from under us as a planet, our individual fate will be determined by the level to which we have evolved.*

We need to realize the truth behind the powerful pharmaceutical companies that have infiltrated government, technology, schools, media, and regulatory agencies. The truth is coming out of their lies and deceit that perpetuate human harm.

A great example has been reported by Jon Rappaport. In an article that Jon wrote, "*Drilling down into flu deceptions and mind-boggling lies,*" in November 2019, he spoke about the deceptive reporting by the CDC when they were hyping up the swine flu pandemic in 2009. It turns out that out of the 62,034 cases of 'influenza and pneumonia' that were reported to hype up the population to get regular and swine flu shots, "in only 18 cases was the flu virus positively identified." These figures come from an article in the British Medical Journal by Doshi (*"Are US flu death figures more PR than science?" BMJ 2005; 331:1412*). The point that has come to the light of awareness is that we have believed hype and lies. We need to listen to the people who have done real research into real facts to learn the truth.

We need to pay attention to the actual cases of vaccine damage reported by parents. There is a war on truth when it comes to vaccines and the pharmaceutical industry. They claim to be healing when they are, in fact, killing us. This is supported by the all cause death rates. The death rates did not increase in 2020 during the so-called pandemic, however, they rose dramatically in 2021 after the vaccine rollout operation. They are after profits and mass depopulation. Get the facts. Read the reports. Read the plans. Listen to whistleblowers who have first-hand information. Find out what organizations and agencies are tied into the system of corruption. Follow the money.

Truth Warriors abound these days. I have found many independent journalists on the Internet that have been super educational. The truth resonates with my intuitive sense and inner guidance. My conscience confirms what feels true.

In addition, clear-minded independent thinkers depend on substantiated facts, not opinions, rumors, or narratives. There are plans from institutions, articles in medical journals, actual statistics, patents with explanations that reveal intentions, and actual quotes from people who are involved in the agendas. Critical thinking is essential.

All of the puzzle pieces fit together. There is hard evidence. Personally, I think God is cleaning house. With our higher frequencies of light, we are attuned to truth and we are accelerating our *power of discernment.*

We are pure and innocent, in a way, and yet we have this new element of consciousness that detects deceit, agendas, and motives. In our shift to higher consciousness, we resonate with only the higher frequencies of truth.

We are at a fork in the road of life. We have a choice to shift our consciousness and live, or go down the primrose path of deception and group think and perish. If we are humble enough, we can release what we once believed to be true and open to new information. Once we become aware of where we are/were headed, we can change directions, ascend to a new consciousness, and heal our lives and our planet.

We have to be independent thinkers. We need our inner powers of perception. We can't afford to NOT evolve.

As we become Self-Realized, accessing our Source within, becoming Love—we will survive and thrive. Are you ready for the passage?

At the very least, take off the blinders, step back and look at the bigger picture, and BE AWARE.

Are you aware of these new trends?

- Eugenics and depopulation agendas and operations
- Vaccine deaths and injuries
- A rise in autism
- An increase in Alzheimer's
- Geoengineering-caused atmospheric anomalies
- Weather manipulation
- Personal surveillance and fusion centers
- Agenda 21/2030 land and resource acquisitions
- The Georgia Guidestones

- Use of DEWs (Directed Energy Weapons)
- Increased cancer, including a sharp rise in childhood cancer
- Fires and health problems caused by smart meters
- Surveillance by tech companies and their relationship to big pharma
- Weaponized technologies including AI, transhumanism, and the IOT (the Internet of Things)
- Suppressed free energy technologies
- Suppressed healing technologies
- An increased awareness of extraterrestrial presences
- "Captured" agencies such as FCC, FDA, EPA, etc.
- Globalist banking and control schemes (World Economic Forum)
- False flags or engineered events that harm or frame innocent people
- Fabricated or staged "appearances" used by media to deceive viewers
- Worldwide EXPOSURE of corruption, censorship, and mind control

These are not things that you will find on television or in the newspaper, for the most part. Those are tools of those who wish to control public perception. Primarily, they support disease and war. If you don't see past the sugar coating of deceptive language and advanced mind control techniques, then you might not have opened the Treasure Box of truth jewels. You can find much information on the Internet, but you have to search. You have to know where to look. You can follow the independent researchers that are helping to increase awareness of the truth by digging up information that showed up and was brushed aside or scrubbed at some point.

Likely, you are already aware of these things since you are reading or listening to this book. And if you are, you are certainly meant to help other awakening souls. You have already been evolving. You are qualified and prepared for the next phase of human evolution. Your soul has been activated.

When we are grounded in the kingdom of the soul and live through our heart, we are attuned to truth. Then, our inner knowing gives us the feelings that endorse the truth, like truth chills. And conversely, we may get feelings of yuck that make us know there is something not resonating with truth. Cognitive dissonance can be used as a tool for discernment.

> *Solutions exist.*
> *It is our responsibility to discover and implement them.*

Now it's time to wake up and help remind each other of our true nature. Therein lies our personal power. It's time to become aware of what Life is all about and how it works. It is evident looking at our personal affairs and our world situation that we've discovered what doesn't work.

We are *finally* ready to stop playing victim and take responsibility for our own experiences. We are, at last, ready to bend our knee to the Higher Intelligence of the Universe (whatever you wish to call this in your personal vernacular) and see that if we are not in tune with God's laws of love, we cannot create a harmonious and peaceful existence. We are breaking cycles of limitations and abuse. We are now realizing the subtle mistakes we have made. At last we see that we are here to give rather than to take.

With the realization of our personal power we can move forward with a strong sense of hope. We can hope for the best possible outcome for our lives and for our planet.

Hope is the seed of achievement. Upon hope we build our faith. Our faith indicates what we believe is possible. Once we can believe something is possible then we can create it, for as the saying goes "What we can conceive, we can achieve."

Divine Purpose and Using Challenges as Opportunities for Evolution

The things that we are discovering in our world that is wrong, the things that cause destruction to our planet and damage to our health, the things that prevent each person from fulfilling their basic needs, and the things that go against natural human rights of freedom— these things we can use as catalysts for our evolution. We are evolving at every level: mind, body, heart, and soul.

It seems that Divine Purpose is behind it all. It's all energy that is calling to be transcended, transmuted, and transformed.

WE are being alchemized. We are changing fundamentally. Since we are connected by the ethers, we are shifting collectively as we transform individually. We are part of one great field of light—the consciousness that generates what comes into form.

All of these inspired ideas from so many people are accumulating, coalescing, and percolating. The seed of humanity is ripening. We are birthing the next race of humans as we evolve. We are stretching our abilities and expanding our expressions to full our divinity. As souls, we are flowering.

The Great Awakening is Underway!

I can see that the world *is* waking up now. We are here to remind each other that we are all One, and together we create our global reality. Everything that we do for ourselves affects everyone else in the world. This is so true.

The result of our behavior affects the whole. It's like when you throw a stone in a lake and wave circles keep rippling outward from where the stone went into the water. We are actually part of an energy system and the energy travels spherically, like outward from a ball.

Is energy real? Nothing exists apart from it. But we can't see energy! (Oh, no! It can't be real!!) Nothing exists without energy and our old belief system told us that only what we see is real. It must be time for a perception adjustment because we now know that this just isn't true.

Now we are discovering the real reality, the unseen behind the seen. What is inside of us is cause and what we experience on the outside, all of our experiences and our physical world, are effect.

We can create any kind of reality that we want. We just have to understand the principles of how to create, and then apply those principles consciously. We've already been creating. We've created the world such as it is, but we notice there is room for improvement.

Since we are all one, it is most powerfully beneficial to share our intentions and visions. My hope is to inspire a unified consciousness of peace, love, joy, and harmony so we can create positive global changes that result in a better life for everyone with a clean and healthy planet.

I have a personal vision and a global vision, and they are much the same.

For my personal vision, I am choosing to create my life to be full of peace, harmony, and love. I choose to be healthy and happy. I choose to use my creative energy to produce wonderful things that would benefit humanity. I choose to experience abundance. I choose to express from the essence of who I am: Love. I choose to benefit everyone whose life I touch. I intend that this is so. I envision it with powerful love. You can do the same for yourself. If you were drawn to this book, you probably already are.

For my world vision, I look out at the world and see all of humanity experiencing such a life—one full of abundance, peace, harmony, and love. I'm holding the vision of everybody working in harmony with nature and I see a clean and beautiful earth. In my image of the perfect outcome, I see everyone enjoying expressions of love, sharing and caring. I see everyone celebrating in joy that we've learned how to create such an existence. I know this is possible. I have faith that we're on our way and it's unfolding right now.

Where Do *You* Stand?

What are you feeling about the condition of the world today? Are you feeling fearful? Are you feeling helpless? Are you attempting to take action by signing Internet petitions or getting involved in political activities? Or are you so beset with your own personal challenges, such as finances, health, or relationship issues that the world conditions take a back seat in your activities? What are your discussions like with your friends and family? Is the general tone that of excitement and hope or that of fear, helplessness, or discouragement? Are you managing energies to keep the peace?

For most of us, it is an ever-changing combination of thoughts and feelings as we move through these unprecedented times. Either way, we are observing that there are many layers of challenges to solve to create a better life experience. I'm telling you right now things can change fast for the better, for you personally—and for the whole world.

We have more power than most of us realize. Let us become aware of our powerful latent abilities and band together and use the strength of unity to create positive change now.

It *is* possible to feel empowered: to really feel and know that you are having a powerful beneficial effect on the world and those around you. This book contains vital information that if applied by large numbers of people, could radically and rapidly change our world for the better. No matter how many people actually apply this information, the effects will be powerful and effective. Our world and our personal lives will be better.

I feel a lot of gratitude for each of you who apply these principles of truth, as does God and the rest of humanity for the beneficial impact you have.

We don't fully realize our personal power because our perception has been, up until now, that our reality stems from the outside physical world. Indeed, to many, it still seems that way.

I am now inviting you, no matter where you are in your field of awareness, to take up your weapons of truth, knowledge, and spiritual wisdom and feel the strength of peaceful empowerment. Deep inside you have latent abilities that once reminded of them, you can practice and utilize once again. Please read this with an open mind and heart. Be prepared to put your personal tools and abilities into action. Be prepared to join the team of caring, loving souls who wish to make positive changes now. You are being activated!

Please be aware that I am speaking to many people here with a wide range of levels of awareness. My attempt is to keep this information simple and basic, even though many are already on the path of applying and embodying this wisdom, in order to explain our abilities that we aren't accustomed to using or even talking about. Also, forgive me if I use words that trigger negative connotations for you. Please look beyond the language and receive the essence of the communication; hear it and discern whatever truth it holds for you.

I honor and respect each person, as we are all equals: unique and significant to the operation of our human life system. You are honored for playing your part.

The Alchemy of Humanity

Change your Self; change the world.

Alchemy was formerly thought to be magical. Now that energy transformation is beginning to be understood, we can grasp that it only takes the proper recipe to transform the consciousness of the planet.

The age-old saying in alchemy is "as above, so below; as below, so above." This truth brings about the realization that as we change ourselves, we are changing the world. As we become aware of our own inherent creative powers and begin to use them consciously, we come to realize how much of a difference every single individual can make. With a new understanding of how we naturally use quantum physics to create our reality from within, we realize that we can easily move from fear to love and make the changes that we all desire.

Life is a system of energy. Since energy cannot be created nor destroyed (The Law of Conservation of Energy), we can understand that we can change our lives by transforming our personal energy within. As we apply the wisdom of alchemy, "as above so below," we realize when we change ourselves, we change the world. Love is the alchemical agent that can be used for this transformation. This means we can bring peace to our lives and our planet right now by fully learning how to love.

Love is the alchemical ingredient that can be applied practically in our daily lives. This means we can bring peace to our lives and our planet right now.

We all have free will. Although we may use our will to make choices for ourselves, it is not ethical or desirable to force our will to make choices for others. People who attempt this soon realize they are wasting their energy, because in the long run, everyone ultimately chooses their own course in life.

Since all people have free will choice, the idea of controlling others is obsolete. We are destined to control ourselves through our inner navigational soul instrument of conscience. We KNOW what is and isn't right because we KNOW what is and isn't love. In our planetary evolution, we are replacing attempts to control others to a consciousness where we are operating at the vibrational frequency of the Absolute truth of love whereby we control ourselves. This dissolves the abuses of power. Exposure of those who violate Universal Law by trying to control or harm others is up front and center. As we awaken, we do not allow oppressive and harmful energies, or people who carry such energies, to overreach their prerogatives of personal power. There is no authority greater than God who has granted us individual sovereignty. In our awakening, we are becoming aware of motives that do not stem from love.

The first thing you can do is to offer hope to your fellow humans as you regain your personal power. Just by instilling hope in your own being, you emanate it for others.

Education

> "Ultimately, the problems of cities and the environment, of production and consumption, and of crime, health, and world peace are educational problems."
>
> Seven Words That Can Change the World
> Joseph R. Simonetta

Everyone is both a teacher and a student. We each have our perspective of what we view of the whole life experience and the truth we have discovered, and although we see different things based on our relative position and experiences, we are *all* right.

Listening to other points of view expands our awareness and we learn. What every single person has to say is important because they convey a piece of the puzzle that forms together to make the whole. Listen wholeheartedly to others and intend to understand the essence, the pure truth that the communication holds for you.

We teach as we share our own perspective. We are each very rich with information that can help serve each other and the whole of humanity. Let's apply what we learn and walk our talk.

Education begins with self-awareness. We are unique and individual while being connected as a whole simultaneously. Heart-centered wisdom comes from self-awareness. We are now learning that fostering and supporting individual talents, gifts, strengths, and skills is the path of true education.

We need to teach each one control of self, development of self, and the value of self. The vibrational field where souls thrive is one of unconditional love and wise guidance. As each one strives to be their best, they create a model as an example for others to follow. They create patterns of thinking than can be transferred to others. Patterns of behavior that demonstrate giving, helpfulness, and kindness ripple out to affect the whole. These patterns of goodwill affect the mental and feeling world of others. They heal. They are replicated. They effect positive change.

Our current failing educational institutions are weaponized to produce group think and minions that obey false narrative against the grain of the conscience. These institutions will transform or dissolve. They have underestimated the power of the light within each soul. They have underrated the resilience of inner intelligence. They are now reckoning with this massive awakening and realizing that justice prevails in a universe built on mathematical energetic vibrational balance.

Love is the highest and most powerful energy vibration. Love generates peace and the comprehension of truth. The system itself is miraculous. One has to be deluded to not recognize the power of love and truth, but many have been. Others have been led astray.

Joy to the World

Won't it be fun to change our own little world? We can change the tone of conversations by injecting messages of hope. We can help open people's minds up with the power of love and laughter. We can help eliminate illusory or self-imposed limitations with simple reminders. We can remember and trust that Divine intervention is only a prayer away. We can trust in the perfect process of life. We can create joy wherever we go.

Let's lighten up and laugh a lot during the course of the reconstruction of our world. We have some work to do, but we can have lots of fun and enjoy each other in the process. We're already doing it in many areas. Let's just keep sharing with each other and expanding our field of impact to reach the masses. Let's envision that everyone is living in joyful abundance, sharing love and creative expressions.

Let's create the space for creative freedom. Crush the censorship and powers that thought they were in control. Practice civil disobedience when laws that clearly go against the grain of conscience are implemented. Don't participate in systems that are not supporting free will that we are inherently endowed with.

One story I heard recently was about laws that were passed in Dallas, Texas, that made it illegal to feed the homeless. We can be kind and generous as our conscience instructs us to in spite of wrong mandates to the contrary. The laws in Dallas prohibited the feeding of the homeless by requiring paperwork, fees, permits, etc. If you didn't pay money and go through these hoops, you were in violation of the law and could be prosecuted. But a group of people got together and formed a group called "Don't Comply". They set out to feed the homeless without adhering to those ridiculous laws. They used their second amendment rights to bear arms. They carried unconcealed weapons as they gathered together and carried out a plan to feed the homeless. They committed civil disobedience, but they did the right thing.

It takes courage. Inner strength grows when we do the right thing regardless of inimical pressures.

The Sovereign Soul Dominion

The Kingdom of God is within the heart. As we place attention within and sense our innermost being within our heart, we find that we are Universal love. We are the Christ of God. We reflect the pure, clear image of God. This is how we attune to God. We are one with God in vibration, pure love. We are Spirit.

Our human evolution consists of the vibration of universal unconditional love taking over our entire being as we seek the truth of our own Divinity. We are on our knees in humility as we seek God, and Absolute Truth, with innocence and sincerity. Our faith grows as we cultivate the relationship with spirit within.

As we persevere through life, using our spiritual connection to answer questions, overcome difficulties, and provide creative inspiration, our sense of self changes.

While the outer world and people in it may influence us toward our lower nature—where we identify with our body and the physical world—our inner world is lifeward. It is where we identify as our True Self, or spirit. Our True Self is Eternal. We have a blueprint for perfection.

During our journey through a human incarnation, the evolving soul transmutes the lower self into the qualities and essence of the higher self. One's ideals change along the way.

The initial journey may be circumscribed by individual wants and needs, and a drive toward material gain and physical pleasure may prevail. However, as we develop we raise our vibration to love and learn to give and to serve and it does our heart good to provide for the welfare and happiness of others. We shift from service to self to service to others.

What make us happy fundamentally changes. Our consciousness expands. When we realize the oneness of all life and connection through breath—The Holy Spirit—we enjoy the Oneness of Spirit through the vibration of love where knowledge is directly perceived. We are literally one with Absolute Truth, which is Light—consciousness itself.

When Jesus said: "I and My Father are one," he was demonstrating this consciousness. He is our pattern of perfection. "Follow me." As we follow the precepts of Jesus, our consciousness transforms. Love is not a concept; it is the vibratory field of consciousness known as Heaven.

"Heaven is within." Deep in each and every heart are the treasures of the soul. Through prayer and meditation, regularly and continuously, we reach higher states of being and our soul takes dominion over the physical-material realm.

With the soul in dominion, sovereignty is established. In the Kingdom of Heaven, the consciousness creates reality. We become conscious creators attuned to the will of God and we express our soul's blueprint and reach our highest potential.

Lower vibrational beings either don't have souls, or they don't know their True Self and they are not identified, or attuned, to the truth of spirit. They have to deceive, trick, and steal. But souls who are evolved and know that their True Self Divinity is dominant over these phantoms of the night can use their knowledge of their inherent sovereignty to rule over the lower beings, just as we have learned to rule over our lower selves.

The essential nature of sovereign souls is the Love of God that shines the Light of Truth. Each soul IS that eternal light, and so lies, secrets, and dark deeds are revealed.

Right now, we are coming into our own sovereignty, individually and collectively. We are ousting the little devils that once called themselves politicians, judges, government officials, corporate executives, priests, regulatory agencies, and other euphemistic titles that covered up their nefarious agendas.

The more we do our inner work of realizing our true identity and eternal essence of Universal love, Christ-lighted consciousness, and calibrate to the will and wisdom of God, then the more our outer conditions reflect that. We are moving toward perfection. We are creating Heaven on Earth.

> *Our inner Heaven becomes our outer reality.*

Chapter Two

THE PERFECTION OF IT ALL

> *Everything is perfect right now.*
> *We can realize this with the highest perspective.*

On Earth As It Is In Heaven

Did you ever wonder what heaven was like? Why do people say "heavenly skies?" Have you ever heard "all the stars in heaven?" When people exclaim that an experience is "heavenly," they seem to feel like nothing could be better. What about in the Lord's Prayer where it says "on earth as it is in Heaven," what does that mean?

It probably means something different to everybody, but I'm going to suggest something. Perhaps it means that we are meant to shine our light upon the world as we become like the stars in heaven.

At the time of our physical death we have accumulated a host of life experiences in which people have affected us and we have affected other people. If we are conscious, those experiences have resulted in personal evolution. That means that at the soul level we have become better.

> *"For all we do in life, for all we have, for all the places we go, things we see, relationships we have, jobs we do, when all is said and done, all we take with us when we leave is what we have become."*
>
> *"It IS A New World After All:*
> *Poetry & Prose to Inspire A New World Vision"*
> *Michelle Marie Angel*

Becoming is a process as is life. Life is the process of becoming. More and more people are becoming aware of that. Spiritual awakening involves a process of going into the inner realms of Self and realizing our true nature—our talents, our gifts, our strengths, our connectedness with Divine wisdom, our soul purpose—and then expressing our highest selves to the outside world. This is the process that makes the light of our soul shine ever brighter. This is the process that brings joy to our lives and benefits the world in our own unique way.

There are many ways to explore the inner Self. Meditation puts us in touch with All That Is—the God within us—and helps us to keep our Self in harmony and to access Divine wisdom and love. The more we meditate, focusing our attention on God in our hearts and minds, the more we experience peace. Not only do we find peace when we meditate, but it can stay with us as we carry on our day.

Alternatively, we can feel our soul essence by being out in nature. We resonate with nature as we tune in to pure spirit. The ground, sky, fresh air, sunshine, water, animals, birds, butterflies, trees, flowers, grass, plants, rocks, gems, minerals—all carry the vibration of spirit and we can commune with that energy as intelligent life giving spirit. We feel the peace of God, or Universal love. Our inner lake is stilled through vibration resonation and it's a perfect time to just BE. It's also wonderful to reflect, contemplate, and absorb the cosmic wisdom direct from prana—essential life energy.

Another type of inner experience is asking questions of our souls such as "Who am I?", "Why am I here?", and "What is my purpose?"

We can ask our souls anything about our true nature and the answer will come. Additional inquiries may include: "What does my soul's blueprint look like?" or "How does my soul plan fit into God's Divine Plan?" "Who are my guides?" "What is the purpose for this particular experience or challenge that I am facing right now?" "What does God want me to know?"

We can observe ourselves, checking to see if we are living up to our highest ideals. Reflection is observation after the fact. We can use it to see where we might have thought, said, or done something different—a little better. Or we can use it to check our overall state of being in every aspect: heart-relationships, mind-career, body-health, and soul-spiritual development as displayed by our personality or essential beingness.

We have inner experiences all the time, even when we don't do it consciously. Our gut feelings are communications from our soul. These feelings tell us if we resonate with a particular way of being in terms of what we might say, or what we might do, or a decision we might make.

Intrinsic value is the warm feeling of resonation we get when we are expressing in tune with our soul. This is soul verification and it is good. We feel a love for ourselves inside for an accomplishment born of love. The Christ Light within develops our conscience. Our conscience is the greater wisdom that is an accumulation from being in tune with Spirit.

We can ask ourselves as we contemplate our expressions, have I come from fear or have I come from love? Am I being reactive, or am I being creative? Am I operating from the perspective of Oneness Awareness, or from separation? The best thing to do is to "respond" after processing within with the greatest wisdom and gentle kindness. Wise honest communication is imperative in our new way of evolved being.

We have become programmed with an old paradigm model with belief systems and values that we have used to unconsciously select our reactions from, and they have become habitual. We have thought patterns that have been reinforced by the social programming of the masses. Seeing the overall picture of where we have been, in terms of consciousness, to where we are going helps us in our self-reflective assessment. There is no judgment of our self, just an essence of a parent lovingly raising a child to a higher understanding of life. Unconditional Love, including Self, is essential to our waking up process.

In the new paradigm, we realize our Oneness of spirit and seek to become ever more loving. We bring up our old stuff (fears and defense reactions) and process that through our new realization and our new creation of our idea of the highest version of our self. We watch our self and catch old patterns emerging. The first step is just to notice. The next step is to change within our minds and hearts how we wish to be in specific circumstances and in general. The next step is to express the pure essence of our soul outwardly in our thoughts, words, and actions.

> *The love in your heart is your shining star,*
> *and it's who you truly are!*
> *Shine far!*

To expedite this process, we can go through an intense period of self-awareness and self-clarification. There are many workshops and self-practices that can facilitate this process. I have my own set of activities that I share in my workshops. But these processes, to be most effective need to be ongoing. One great way is to use workbooks such as the *Bulls-Eye Faith Inner Workbook*, and the *Wake Up Workbook* to do exercises that promote personal contemplation.

In my work, I spawn visioning support groups where people get clear on their intentions and create detailed visions of the essence of the outcome that they are consciously creating. These folks continue to support each other as they implement the truths that they have gleaned from workshops and life to become more fully expressive of their own unique expression of their true nature. These support groups perpetuate the group synergy of the workshops that give us such a "high" feeling. It really doesn't have to end when the workshop is over. It is a great way to shift to a more intentional way of creating life experiences.

At the same time, personal ongoing practices, such as meditation, quiet walks in nature, creating inner moments throughout the day, and awareness practices also stimulate ongoing personal evolution. They also keep us present in the moment and in touch with who we are so that we can be always truly authentic.

Heaven is certainly within, but with an ongoing expansion of awareness, is can just as well be without—fully felt and displayed in our outer life as well. We can create our own heaven on earth. Individuals change and the whole world changes. This is happening. We are indeed in the process of creating Heaven on Earth.

Perception

Perception is our understanding or awareness of a given thing. It is our knowledge obtained through the senses and the filters of the mind. Unless we believe in infinite possibilities, our beliefs are the filters that may limit what we perceive or know.

Our expansiveness of awareness determines the level of our sensory perceptions such as seeing, or hearing. For example, when it comes to our sight, our vibratory rate determines what range that we can see in the electromagnetic spectrum.

Soul perception accessed by going within deepens our perception to reach an inner knowledge of truth. It is beyond the mind. It extends through the portal of our heart and expands into the whole of spirit. Our heart translates the knowledge of the deep perceptions of our soul through a mechanism of truth acquisition and language interpretation. The language of our soul comes to our mind through our heart's understanding, or comprehension of the light. Its efficacy is developed through practice. Intuition increases and conscience is developed through inner wisdom.

When soul perception is regularly accessed, heart intelligence increases. Heart intelligence has a broader scope as well as increased depth. When heart intelligence becomes dominant in the consciousness, the higher dimensional fields of being become the actual new normal. It establishes a higher baseline state of consciousness. This is what some refer to as they speak of ascension.

The vibrational frequency shifts to a higher degree and more light is radiated through the being from soul light. Illumination occurs. Radiance increases. The soul spark is the center point of our personal electromagnetic field, a fractal in the hologram of consciousness.

The electromagnetic field, or light, is an electric field with a magnetic field moving at 90 degrees to it. The electrical field is moving in a wave and the magnetic field is moving at 90 degrees to this wave, and the whole configuration is rotating as it moves through space.

The light field itself and the eye that receives it are in the same geometric pattern because the receiver has to tune to that which it is receiving.

Vibration is calibrated by the extent of our awareness. It is our vibration that determines what realm of life we perceive. We raise our vibration by expanding our awareness of self. This raises consciousness to a new level where a broader perspective can be realized. This keeps pointing back to the importance of knowing the kingdom of the soul and perceiving our soul identity. Advanced perception is the key. It is realized through inner awareness.

Each experience is colored and created by our inner awareness of perception. Experience expands our awareness. Knowledge expands our experience. True Self perception is the foundation of knowledge and experience.

Perspective

Perspective, on the other hand, is a person's point of view based on their relative position to the thing being viewed. For example, if you are in a park playing on the swing set, you can see the swing and the nearby objects. From the sky you can see the whole park.

While we are living our lives, we have experiences or notice things in our world that don't seem just or loving. We don't always sense the perfection of life. However, from the highest perspective, all *is* perfect.

It's hard to tell someone whose baby or child died that everything is perfect. And yet it is. From the perspective of the grieving parent, things couldn't seem any further from perfect. The depth of emotional pain caused by such a loss is one that never totally diminishes. The question of "why?" echoes through time until one day at last it is discovered...and it will be discovered.

From a higher perspective, we can discover true purpose. When we see with our human eyes, we get a partial view. When we see with our spiritual eye, we get an expanded view. Our spiritual eye isn't limited by appearances. Our spiritual eye can reveal a broader context. It is transcendent. It operates in the realm of the Eternal and Absolute.

Linda, my best friend since childhood, was 46 years old and had cancer when we discussed this issue. I had met her in third grade when we were 8, and she was one of the dearest people in my life. She was the only one who I felt truly understood me completely and accepted me no matter what. And she was always there to help me. We could talk about anything at any level. She was the most spiritually enlightened person I knew besides my grandmother.

She had been fighting cancer for around 6 years as she was raising 3 children. Her youngest, Mitch, was 5. He was the one she was pregnant with when she first discovered she had breast cancer. During those 6 years, she had breast cancer, bone cancer, and lung cancer. Linda experienced a lot of pain. She went through chemotherapy several times, had radical surgery, and tried every kind of healing modality there was.

She called me on a Saturday night to tell me that she wasn't going to fight anymore and that she knew she was going to die. She was telling me that she was sorry to let me down. I told her I was proud of her and reminded her: "You know, Linda, at the highest level, everything is perfect." I also reminded her that she had accomplished a lot and had become so much more as she was learning through the experience of her cancer. I told her that everything that she had become, she takes with her. She thanked me and told me that it meant more to her than words could say. She knew it; she just needed the reminder. She passed 6 days later.

Linda and I were always aware that at that the soul level we had planned all of the challenges in our lives. We used to joke around and say, "What the hell was I thinking when I planned this one?"

We know that there is a reason for everything. Of course, that didn't prevent my grief. There's nothing like losing a best friend. Experiencing such deep sadness makes us feel such compassion for those who have lost loved ones.

> **When we just keep asking:**
> **"What am I learning from this experience?"**
> **we get our answers, evolve our souls,**
> **and Divine Purpose is served.**

At the same time, the awareness that it's a matter of perspective helps us to understand the meaning of our life experiences. When we just keep asking: "What am I learning from this experience?" we get our answers, evolve our souls, and Divine Purpose is served.

We can be grateful for the purpose of each experience. We can thank God for the richness of Life and the resulting wisdom that becomes part of our soul. We can move ever closer to the expression of our Divine Potential. An understanding of Life and its Purposes keeps us in the high vibration of gratitude and love.

A God's-Eye View

Life is a process—a perfect flow of energy that abides within Universal Law.

Everything is perfect right now. Divine Order is a Universal Truth that exists eternally. No matter what we perceive or see that is happening in our world, remember one thing: *Everything works together for the good of God.* That's Divine Order.

God and *love* and *life* are synonyms. Try repeating *Everything works together for the good of God*, and have a personal contemplation moment. Feel it into your soul and feel the healing power that truth contains. That will change your perspective! And with deep contemplation, applying it to a certain situation in your life, peace and wisdom will come to soothe your heart and mind.

If we had a God's-Eye view of what's happening in any given moment, we would have our own realization that everything *really is* perfect. When I feel resistance, I will ask within: *"What's perfect about this?!?"* I have received deeply profound and elaborate answers in the silence of meditative inquiry.

Picture the spiral of a galaxy. From the core emanates matching spirals of darkness and light. But look at the tails of both the dark and the light spirals. The darkness disappears into infinity. This dissipation indicates an absence of energy, or death. (Of course, there is no real death. There is no beginning and no end, just transformation of energy.) Conversely, the light expands and moves on to create new stars and suns and galaxies. It indicates an expansion of life.

Divine Purpose

Each cycle within life is laced with Divine Purpose. When we align ourselves with Divine Purpose, we are in the flow of evolving life. The flow of evolution is characterized by bonding and unity. The darkness dissipates as the light bonds together. As a result of unified energy, the light increases its luminosity.

When we don't align ourselves with Divine Purpose, or direct our energy constructively, we tend toward de-evolution. The flow of de-evolution is characterized by entropy and chaos. As a result of the chaos, the light dissipates and looks like darkness.

De-evolution within has to do with the undermining of conscience. The intelligence, or light within our hearts and souls, is diminished or ignored. We fall prey to rationalization or social programming that says something is all right, when it's not. It is extremely important to consciously connect to the light within, the Divine connection with Spirit that guides us to our highest good when we pay attention to it. This connection is the treasure of all treasures!

Cycles are circular. The beginning and the end are all at the same point. However, at the end of the cycle we either progress up or down the spiral like an elevator.

We all have free will. There is no judgment. Choices that promote life, love, and unity lead us into the light. Choices that promote fear, destruction, and chaos lead us into the dark.

Remember that childhood game when we hid something and had someone go find it? When they were getting closer, we would say: "you're getting warmer!" When they went farther away, we would say: "you're getting colder." Think of the truth in that. Love is warm and leads us to more life.

When people express their True Selves, Love, they are said to be "warm" and "loving" or "caring" and "gentle" and "kind". When people are not expressing this type of nature, they are said to be "cold" and "uncaring" and "selfish".

When we are consciously evolving, all choices bring about greater awareness. As we notice the cause and effect of what we say, think, and do, we realize how to make choices that are constructive or lead to evolution. We can feel what brings us into light or darkness by feelings of love or fear. All forms of love feel warm, expansive, and unifying; all forms of fear feel cold, contracting, and separating.

With the acceptance that each soul has free will to choose what path it takes, we can be at ease knowing that Divine Order is in place. Every choice will either lead toward unity with the whole, or separation—the choice between light and darkness. Love is Light. Light is Truth. We unify around Love and Truth. It is magnetic!

When we are attuned to and navigate with the love in our hearts, we inherently gravitate toward unity. We like what is warm; what feels good. When we are not attuned to love, separateness prevails. So we will get closer and closer to those who shine the love from their core, and farther and farther from those that don't come from love. Universal organization is natural.

The bottom line is, although everything is perfect, we ultimately create our individual destinies by our own individual choices. As humanity, we choose our destiny by cooperating in unified consciousness.

As we will discuss further, being attuned to Spirit, deriving our Will from God's Will, and operating with pure hearts and open minds, we live lives of conscious intentions. We direct our attention first to our core, then in an outward Expression of Pure Divinity. We become perfect instruments of Divine Harmony through attunement-inspired conscious intentions-alignment of thoughts, words, feelings, and deeds—and expression of our highest Divine Potential. The perfect recipe for living in Joy and Peace!

Our Soul's Journey

The essence of our true nature is our soul, or our spiritual aspect. Our souls evolve by having a series of life experiences. There is a divine reason for *absolutely everything*. With an understanding that we are part of a whole life system and that we created this life experience with purpose, we tune in to our souls via our Higher Self within and we become clear about why we are here and what we are up to.

There are many layers of purpose. Each of us are evolving as souls and simultaneously evolving the whole. Generally, we are all evolving toward love, our Source and the essence of who we are. Specifically, we all have planned lives to balance our experiences so that we can see each type of understanding that we've picked from both sides.

For example, in one lifetime, we may be the perpetrator of insult such as rape. In another lifetime, we choose to be the victim of rape. Or we may have persecuted homosexuals in one lifetime, and in another lifetime we have the experience of being a persecuted homosexual. It serves our soul's awareness and evolution. Our understanding must be complete to become the full expression of unconditional love for all.

Karma is just about balancing actions and experience, but not all life experiences are related to karma. Sometimes we choose life experiences to develop an understanding for a soul skill that we are developing. We use our experiences to become really good at something, or to specialize. There are many reasons we choose our life experiences, but they all have purpose.

There have been several hypnotherapists who discovered the nature of our soul's path through regressing clients back to pre-birth existence and to their bardos, the soul's life between lifetimes. By examining the life processes and asking direct questions of these souls, these therapists have separately discovered the same truths.

Not all people believe in reincarnation, but the statistical evidence is that over 70% of the population believes in life after death. Whatever your belief is, if you stay open to possibilities, the truth will become evident.

Basically, when we die we are greeted by a guide or a loved one and are escorted to a place where we can get energetically revitalized and re-acclimated to our spiritual home. Then we have a life review before a council of elders where we check out how we did. Our guides usually accompany us. *There is no judgment.* It's all just about learning. We remember what we planned on accomplishing in our former lifetime, and we measure how we did with Universal feelings. In other words, we feel all emotional impacts of our behavioral choices. *We* decide how we did by how much we accomplished our soul's intentions for that lifetime. We view scenes of helping or harming others in order to feel from the other's point of reference and we learn from that.

We are each members of a soul group containing about 15 to 25 other souls. We hang out with these souls, go to classes, and have many celebrations. We have jobs to do there, too, if we choose.

There are many things to do in our spiritual home. We love it there! There are a tremendous variety of experiences, places, and souls to experience.

Much of our spiritual home experiences depend on our level of evolution. For example, most of us are greeted by someone as we cross over, but the seasoned soul may just go alone to the first soul stop.

When we and our guides mutually agree that is time, we begin planning our next incarnation. We do this in conjunction with other souls. We select what we want to work on. We go to places like movie houses and check out different family situations, geographical locations, and body types. We choose all of it!

When all of the selections have been made and we are clear about major events and people in our lives, we are given clues to imbed in our consciousness that will make us "click" during our life experience to signify a direction to take or person to connect with. Most of us have a memory of someone or something that we had an uncanny appeal for. We've also had experiences of de-ja vu.

When we get born into our earthly bodies, we go through the "veil of ignorance" so that we don't automatically have all the answers to the tests that we have set up for ourselves. Our tests involve whether we follow old patterns, or begin making higher choices. When we do make higher choices and become better, this is the soul evolution that we intended. Our choices become more love-based and directed toward a larger sense of Self rather than the smaller, egoic sense of self.

While unconscious, we live by trial and error. We repeat the same patterns and get stuck in the mire of life. However, now is the time for awakening, for becoming more conscious about our choices.

When we tune into our souls consciously while incarnated we make the highest choices much more easily. As we develop our souls consciously, the life trials that cause suffering wane and eventually disappear. And when challenges or problems do present themselves, we do it with higher awareness and tools to process the experiences. Love and wisdom bring much peace to our lives. Life becomes a lot more easy and joy-filled.

Pixel Consciousness

On a computer screen, each point of light is a pixel. All of the pixels combined make up the whole picture. Pixel Consciousness is the understanding that we are all part of the same whole unified consciousness. As a human individual, we are each focal points of consciousness with our own perspective. At our core, we are all rays emanating from the same Source, or sphere of consciousness.

With Pixel Consciousness, we can develop an expanded awareness. We have the wisdom to be open to others' points of view as they share their perspective. Although truth passes through the filters of ego and perception, we are designed to discern the truth. As we process perspective communication, we can sort out the truth, just like grain is plucked from the chaff.

Our picture therefore, is not 2D like a computer screen, or even 3D like a sphere, but vast and cosmically comprehensive. There are actually other factors involved that increase the dimensionality as we become attuned.

Pure knowing comes from attunement with God. By being still and silent we can sense the presence of God. In this state we can elicit any answer from the Universe. Our awareness expands naturally. When we realize our Oneness, we see the good, or the God in all. By keeping our attention on what is good about each other, we illuminate the God in each other. It's a great practice that brings peace of mind and deeper love in relationships.

Real Life Application: A Perception Adjustment

Sometimes when I get frustrated in life, I stop and do a *"perception adjustment."* I know everything is perfect, but if I'm bugged about something, it helps me to step back and take a God's-eye view to understand the perfection of the situation.

One such perception adjustment brought me great peace of mind. My teenage son had a room that was so gross—it looked like a cross between a junkyard and a science lab. It was messy to the max and the stuff that was growing out of old used glasses made my stomach turn. Trying to get him to clean it was always a waste of energy—merely exercises in extreme frustration. Once I snuck in there when he was gone and started to clean it, but he came home and I got caught. He felt like his privacy had been invaded. He was mad!

I decided to make a perception adjustment. I realized that his time left living with me was relatively short. I knew I wanted his last few years with me to be loving ones, so I decided just to accept his room as it was. I just asked him to bring in dishes when we ran out. Instead of checking to see if was clean, I told him I would just take pictures of it from time to time and make a motion picture out of it by running the picture frames in fast motion. I figured by the time he turned 25 it would be clean and that would be the happy ending to my movie. We got a great laugh out of making it a joke. Even though adolescence meeting menopause had conspired to help escalate our challenges, we now have deep peace and love in our relationship.

> *A perception adjustment removes all barriers to the flow of love. It brings peace to the heart and soothes the soul.*

Perfection Awareness

We can experience Perfection Awareness if we intend to. It's a matter of perspective. If we shift our perception, we can realize the perfection of everything and relax.

Just knowing that everything is perfect doesn't make it instantly evident. The quicker we attune to that awareness, the more evident it becomes.

A friend of mine was driving me to look for furniture once, just hours before the moving trailer was due back and he had to leave. He took an alternate route instead of the highway and I started to get irritated that he was taking longer than necessary. Then I caught myself and I reminded me that "the perfect thing always happens".

Right after that we came upon a furniture store that was going out of business. In the short time we had left, I bought a sofa, loveseat, washer, dryer, refrigerator, and bed. All for an excellent price!! We used the moving trailer to get the new furniture home, and still got it back on time.

Mindset, beliefs, and expectations: they all came into play to help create a more instantaneous experience of perfection. But even when things seem sad and destructive, there's always a blessing.

Linda and I realized the eternal nature of life. We agreed that we would try to communicate after she was on the other side. Just before her passing we decided to make a code word for continued communication. As I mentioned before, we decided it would be "mud." Linda and another friend had peed their pants in fifth grade, and they used to say: "I fell in the mud" when they talked about it to avoid the embarrassment of others finding out, so I suggested that word. She left her body three days after that.

Since then the sight of mud, or the word mud on signs or in books, or the thought of the word has come up in my mind, and I have felt her presence. The first time was when I flew into Detroit to go to her funeral. I looked out of the airplane and all I could see was mud. I laughed as I cried. We still have a relationship even though we are living in different realms. I wrote a poem for her that I read at her funeral called *Forever Friends*, and we truly are.

Divine Purpose

Even if we don't see the perfection or blessing in any given moment or circumstance, we can be sure that Divine Purpose underlies everything. If we ask God for the reason, or purpose behind anything, we will find our answer. Just knowing this truth helps ease our hearts and minds.

Chapter Three

WHAT IS REAL?

Everything is Energy – Do We Believe What We Perceive?

From a scientific perspective, we use our sense of observation and the tools of perception to translate our observations into a system of data collection from which we form our beliefs. If we use only our physical senses of taste, touch, sound, sight, and smell, then our perceptions form from the material realm.

From a spiritual perspective, we also observe energy as feelings, inspired ideas, realizations, and a sense of inner knowing. These perceptions come from a deeper base of observation.

In addition we receive frequencies of thought transference, vibrational attunement or entrainment, and conscious or unconscious changes to our personal energy field that can alter our perceptions.

As we evolve and become more conscious, we monitor our field and discriminate as to which vibrational frequencies resonate with us. We determine and learn to control what vibrational frequency we attune to rather than being subject to outer influences.

The Physics of Energy and the Nature of Feelings

It was not so long ago, when we believed that only what we could observe in our outer world, our physical reality, was real. "Seeing is believing!" was the phrase we used to indicate proof of reality.

Reality was based on our beliefs, or interpretations, of what we experienced. Our beliefs are mental constructs that may or may not be in alignment with absolute truth.

For example, there was a time when most believed in a materialistic science based on physical reality alone. Things needed to be seen and felt and perceived with physical senses to be thought of as valid reality. It had to be measured and tested with physical senses. The physical senses were augmented by tools such as microscopes, telescopes, and meters, etc. Stuff *had* to be physically observed and measured!

Furthermore, the former scientific view of life took on separate forms and characteristics even though life itself is one in its wholeness. The disciplines of psychology, religion, philosophy, mathematics, and science were all seen as separate. Now as truth emerges, the tenets of each discipline are beginning to integrate. The bonds bring all the sciences together to display the one truth behind the separated parts.

No longer are people with HSP (higher sensory perception) being scoffed at or ridiculed. Intuition and imagination have increased validity by many degrees. People with HSP are respected rather than discounted. Their skills that were developed, although once thought of as superstitious or quackery, became more and more respected and valued. And now new fields of endeavor are blooming and innovative ideas are coming into fruition as viable solutions and guiding lights. Even intuitive truth is taking a stand.

Instead of experiencing the dual notion of "this" *or* "that," we are now accepting paradoxical data as being part of the same whole. We can cognize and realize "both/and" inclusiveness. We have not only our outer senses to appreciate and use, but also more and more we are delving into the inner perceptions where truth is known and stable, rather than accepting false or ever-changing beliefs. And most importantly, we are rejecting the narratives that have become part of the mind control deception program. We have learned to develop discernment.

Now scientists are willing to concede to subtle energy forms that are perceived by our inner senses. Our own subtle energy fields are being acknowledged. Quantum physics and metaphysics are blending to realize, explain, and utilize the essential nature of life. We are moving to a more organic whole systems approach.

> *We know real reality by tuning in to intuitive, direct perception of truth that is resident in our hearts.*

Perception of Reality

The overwhelming majority of our population has focused their attention outwardly toward outer physical reality. This picture of seemingly solid objects, liquids, and gases, were perceived to be the total reality. Our minds were shaped by our environment, what we experienced culturally, and what we were told to believe.

Our hearts lost touch with our souls. Our minds became disengaged from our hearts. Inner wars and lack of peace were reflected outwardly. With a lack of awareness of how we use our personal life energy, we thought everything was outside of us. Things were happening *to* us. Sure, we could work and live according to the rules and beliefs that were set before us to make a difference in the world or in our lives. But the vast energy that is our most powerful aspect of self was diminished, often leaving us suffering or feeling hopeless against our circumstances.

Truly we didn't fully understand how our minds worked or what all they could do. Our concept of reality was that everything was "out there," including what we formed in our minds to be the concept of our own identity! Our perceptions were primarily coming from outside of us; from the outer sense information relays filtered by our beliefs. We didn't realize we had any control whatsoever of what our minds were being used for. Therefore, we got used. Part of the mind control was the presentation of "appearances" to our consciousness that were concocted by untrue stories and staged false flags. Our vibration was lowered to fear where it could more easily manipulate our perception of reality. Many a person, religion, and government have been using means to disempower our inherent ability to recognize truth. We've been routinely programmed, or brainwashed, to fulfill personal agendas of others, often based on greed or power.

Internal sensations, such as emotional feelings, were often disregarded. Even when they were acknowledged, they weren't seen for their true inherent value. Feelings were to be concealed, denied, suppressed, or controlled rather than heeded. I acknowledge that when we disregard true deep feelings, we deny God.

Truly we would hit the breaking point and cry to God for help. We didn't know that God was speaking to us all along through our feelings. But we judged our own feelings. We lost our ability to interpret the light of wisdom within the energy of our feelings.

We are just waking up to the fact that feelings contain wisdom. They are the language of our soul. We can tune in to Spirit, or God, through our soul by eliciting the wisdom from our feelings. This information may be the most useful information we can apply in our lives in these times.

This does not eliminate the use of our mind; it enhances it. Love and passion from our hearts illuminates the truth and feeds our mind with knowledge and wisdom. The mind can receive pictorial and symbolic messages and information. The mind can transmit messages and information as well. This is telepathy. Silent communication can be remembered, developed, and used consciously.

The mind is an essential part of conscious creation. It is a useful tool. An illumined mind can direct one's energy to reach its highest potential. It can manifest idea energy into physical reality when powered with love.

When our minds and hearts are united, working as one, we are conscious.

When our hearts and souls are aligned with Spirit, and unified with our mind-heart intelligence, we are reborn into the holistic natural essence of Christ Consciousness. Our inner world becomes calibrated with the greater whole.

We are now learning to open our hearts and use our inner senses.

By getting our attention and identity centered in the core of our being, we are waking up to who we truly are.

Appearances are Reflections

We can get lost in the land of appearances. Some mistake appearances for reality. And yet, appearances are all on the outside. They are the reflections of the consciousness within. We create them.

Consciousness operates as light and mirrors. Light from within shines outwardly. Thoughts direct which appearances are portrayed and created into dimensional form. As we "grow up" in consciousness we evolve and take responsibility for all outward appearances.

When someone is truly lost, they assume that their outward "image" or "appearance" is their identity. This is a pseudo-self. It is sometimes referred to as ego. The ego rules the mind when it thinks it is the self and in control. The ego-mind tries to control appearance through manipulating the outer world. It also has the audacity to think it can control others.

The only way these ego-minded people can control others is through deception. They have to provide limitations to self-perception. They cannot control those who are self-realized and know themselves as sovereign souls. There have been a lot of schemes and efforts to control the minds of others over the centuries. The primary tools involve limiting self-perception; controlling attention, manipulating emotional states, and installing their vision of reality that they choose to create.

They must first decrease the sense of self-worth. They perpetuate the limited sense of identity of ego-mind where "appearance" is the most important thing for self-worth, self-esteem, and self-confidence. They work hard to build up the false sense of self. The ego is increased to vanity by flattery. They use many means, such as commercials or ads that promote the idea of a certain type of appearance. They try to define what it means to be successful.

When the mind programming works, egos are blown up and

the individuals they buy into the programs can become full blown narcissists. Some may be corrupted so much that they become sociopaths. These are all of such low vibration, that they may be susceptible to evil-doing. Narcissists and sociopaths become full of avarice. A false sense of power is ignited and fueled. These lower vibrational beings feed on fancy titles, money, greed, and power.

But what happens when the sword of Truth makes its mark? The whole house of cards based on appearances tumbles. It dissolves.

Accountability happens.

> *Justice restores harmony.*
> *Light opens doors.*
> *Love wins.*
> *Why?*

The reason is that appearances are NOT reality. They are reflections. Only love is real.

Direct Connection with Spirit

The key is to turn attention inward. "Be still and know that I am God." "Seek ye first the kingdom of God, and everything shall be added unto you." "The kingdom of heaven is within." We are now going Home in our hearts to Heaven, to realize how to perceive reality. This is the basis of our gigantic shift. This is what is radically changing how we perceive reality.

> *"It matters not where men abide, on mountain top, in deepest vale, in marts of trade, or in the quiet home; they may at once, at any time, fling wide the door, and find the Silence, find the house of God; it is within the soul."*
>
> Words of Jesus
> The Aquarian Gospel of Jesus the Christ
> by Levi

Everything is energy. It flows from the inside out. We direct our own life energy to create the picture outside of us that we then perceive as reality. Our images married to vibrational feelings create the field which yields our experiences.

It is all energy, the energy of consciousness. Consciousness is electromagnetic—love is magnetic and light is electric. Our outer human senses perceive only a small portion of the electromagnetic spectrum. However, our inner senses of perception and interpretation are being activated more and more now. We are experiencing the revelations of light activation, the rising of vibration and the expansion of awareness.

Reality is our perception of consciousness that is existence of life itself. God is the energy—all of it. We have varying capacities of awareness based on our evolutionary gains. The more we raise our thought and expressive vibrations to love, the more awareness we acquire.

Love is the alpha, or beginning of life. Love said: "Let there be light." Love lights the truth in our heart. Life is ever-changing while love is eternally stable. The Universal Law of life is the balance of love. When love creates integration and wholeness, peace is restored. Awareness is not polarized as positive or negative, but it is neutral. As the darkness of unrealized potential blossoms into its fruition, there is only light. And light returns to love. Love is the omega of life.

Since love is the alpha and omega of life, then love is all there is. It is the source and substance that is neither created nor destroyed, but only changes form.

Our individual lives are possible only by the Love, that Divine Spark of God, which is in our hearts flowing from the essence of Spirit—our eternal souls. It is magnetic, holding the universe together. It is intelligent, ordering the universe. No matter how separate anyone thinks they are from God, they are not. Life is not possible without God.

Each of us has this life energy pouring through our hearts. It is a gift from God. We choose what we do with our lives, every moment of every day. We can use our life energy constructively or destructively.

Since balance is the universal law of life energy, the quality and nature of the energy that we project returns to us. "As ye sow, so shall ye reap." We create our own reality.

> *"You can make the ethers serve the carnal self,*
> *or the Holy Self within."*
>
> Words of Jesus
> The Aquarian Gospel of Jesus the Christ
> by Levi

The purest, most simple forms of energy are light and love. The aspects of light are color and shape. We use the imagination function of our mind to shape forms of color and light. The aspects of love are sound and movement. When we express with sound, whether words, noise or music, we attract like vibration, or that level of love. As life moves through us we can act, or move, in ways that are conducive to love and have a beneficial impact on our larger Self. Life is not contained within us, it simply moves through us.

How we use our life energy is determined by how we direct our attention. This in turn determines how we perceive reality and experience the return of energy. We will delve deeper into the conscious direction of attention in Chapter Six.

Inside our heart, at the center of the core of our being, love is pure. It is our true nature that we can perceive as the foundation and substance of reality. This is where we can truly feel our Oneness with God, our Creator and Source of life.

As we shift our attention more and more to this inner light of love, we suddenly experience such fulfillment, such beauty, such ecstasy, that we barely can believe that we lived any other way.

This is involution. It is the basis of evolution and expanded conscious awareness.

The Physics of Energy

Everything is energy. Energy can be as subtle as thoughts or feelings, or it can be as dense as physical objects. Light gives energy qualities or form. We direct the light energy of our consciousness with our attention. Hence the saying "energy flows where attention goes." Therefore, when we think about something, energy goes there and it creatively forms the energy through the light of our consciousness and is built up with the energy of our emotions—our energy in motion.

Thought is the director of energy. Feeling is the energy.

Once we fully realize we are creating with our natural faculties of thought and feeling, we grasp the impact of our personal power. Instead of creating haphazardly or unconsciously, we begin to direct our thoughts deliberately toward our intentional purposes. This is alignment. We will discuss this further in Chapter Eleven.

Until we consciously direct our attention and choose our thoughts and vibrational feelings deliberately with inspired intention, we are pulled to create and draw experiences either from what we fear or from what we believe in. Beliefs can be limiting and they can be constructed from false convictions, or programming. Initially, we can catch ourselves when we start giving attention to our fears, and switch the direction of our attention into our dreams, or what we wish to create as our life experience. Although it takes effort at first, after a while it becomes natural to direct energy on purpose toward our greatest good.

As we become more conscious with the direction of our energy, we can transmute fear or any other negative energy such as anger into love and power to change things. A specific reliable process to do just that will be described later. By being deliberate with our inspired intentions, we can build faith in our dreams and make them come true. Further, by understanding the nature of energy that is our very being, and how to work constructively with our energy resources we become masters by using the light of consciousness to form matter and experiences.

Pure consciousness is Source Energy. It is essentially light, the same thing that physical reality is made of. Physical objects are actually masses of stable light.

When we delve into our own consciousness, such as in quiet meditation, we can access Source Energy and use it to create, or manifest circumstances, events, or physical objects. We do this by combining our inner visual images, or imagination, with our emotions by directing according to our soul-inspired intentions. Intentions that we derive from our soul are inherently charged within the matrix of collective consciousness because they are in alignment with the whole: they are good for one and all. In satisfying our soul's desires through conscious intention, we experience joy and love for ourselves and love others as ourselves.

People are always trying to make themselves happy, but they run into many snags and snares when they don't realize that it is really inner joy that the soul is craving that drives our desires. Happiness, after all, is a state of mind that we can choose when we are consciously directing our thoughts and feelings.

By applying the Law of Conservation of Energy, that is that energy can be neither created nor destroyed, it can only change form, we manipulate energy through alchemy. As energy flows throughout our consciousness, we can transmute any negative energy back into love, its purest form. Then we can direct this energy to a higher purpose through our vision, or image of a higher outcome.

Ironically, although we can always choose states of happiness, it seems like negative energy perceived within as bad feelings or thoughts, causes us unhappiness. We get pulled from our natural feeling of joy and bliss by dissonant, non-resonant energy. A helpful perspective to apply is that everything is consciousness and consciousness itself contains pure wisdom. As we realize that there is wisdom in our feelings, we can elicit the wisdom from them and transmute the energy back into pure love, or Source Energy. This is more alchemy that allows us to "comprehend the light" and change it to positive purposes. In that process we can take the perspective of the observer and manipulate the energy to make the change so that the feeling or emotion doesn't cause any unhappiness, but brings us further joy. In other words, the soul has the power to translate feeling into information.

Here's an example: Once I was feeling anger. I didn't even understand why I was feeling anger, but what was occurring at the time was that my boyfriend was talking to his sister on the phone. Why was I feeling anger? I had learned by this time that processing the energy of feelings in inner silence would elicit information. I went and sat down in my meditation chair. I just sat with the feeling. The information came: "There is a secret, and your soul wants you to know about it." Wow! Really? I went to my boyfriend and told him what I had perceived. He responded: "Ok, since you are so intuitive, I'll tell you the secret." And he did. I felt relieved of the anger. He probably felt a burden had been lifted as well as he expressed the truth. It really wasn't that big of a deal. It was just something that he thought if I knew it would compromise our relationship. But the truth only makes relationships stronger.

The Primary Relationship with Self

How does one know the truth? By knowing the true nature of Self. The true nature of Self is Truth. It is Light. Light is born of Love of God. Love of God is natural as one places attention on the core of Being, the Inner Light. To know anything, you have to BE it. To BE it, you give attention to it, love it, magnetize it, expand it, and explore it with sincere and humble curiosity and trust. As soon as we can admit we don't know anything, we can know everything. Such is the paradox of life.

The transformation of consciousness is the small self entering the chrysalis of the inner life and emerging as a free actualized spirit of magnificent and most beautiful potential. The butterfly of unique qualities and creative genius emerges and blesses life through daily expression.

One with Truth is One with All. One with Truth is One with Freedom.

The Intelligence of Freedom and the Freedom of Intelligence

The boxes that we as humanity are crawling out of through development of the Inner Light/Inner Life are the illusionary confinements that restrict our greatest intelligence. The infinite intelligence of the universe, or God-Spirit-All That Is, is inherently free. We can accept it, claim it, identify with it, and be free in any given moment.

Infinite intelligence is part of our heart and soul. It exists eternally. But our awareness of our true identity and powers have, to a large degree, been circumvented and restricted. We have been subjected to social programming, inculcation, chemicals that affect our mental capacities (and emotions and physical states of being), and other influences that downplay our awareness of our True Selves.

Freedom is the best gift from God that we can master. We can go into our feeling world and access the feeling of freedom in the peaceful presence of God. We can intend to know our true freedom. We can be free in our Spiritual nature and free the intelligence of our heart, mind, soul, and strength. Isn't this reflective of the greatest commandment expressed by Jesus? "Love your Lord God with all of your heart, mind, soul, and strength." Loving God is a sure mark of a free spirit. A free spirit has awareness of its All-Powerful nature. A free spirit has the Awareness of the power of Free Will. A free spirit knows the Infinite Intelligence and unlimited scope of information recorded in the very ethers where we live and move and have our being. A free spirit knows that there are no limitations of time or space in the inner world of consciousness. A free spirit knows consciousness as cause.

The direct path to knowing is simple: sit still and be receptive. Be humble and ask for information. Tune in to the language of the soul and interpret the information from feelings coming through the heart. Consciously calibrate the consciousness to universal awareness.

This requires a letting go of the identity with mind and body. With mastery, the mind and body become subjective to the indwelling spirit of infinite dynamic intelligence. The whole field is accessible. The Holy Spirit is Truth. Embody the Holy Spirit so that the immanent Christ Light is illumined and stands as King of Consciousness. ***Intuitive knowing prevents the usurpation of freedom through deception.***

True Freedom rests in the mind. Not the mind of the physical brain, but the mind of the soul that is all-inclusive of the Holy Spirit. This is where genius resides. Once the genius is let out of the bottle of restrictive limitations, the soul is free—free to imagine infinite possibilities, free to create, free to be and experience anything. And since it comes through the heart of hearts, it is based in pure love. It knows itself as One with the all. It operates and behaves in such a way to be a beneficial contributor to Life.

Usurpers of God's power of intelligence would turn other humans into subjects and slaves. They would have one think that they are mortal, purely physical beings, reliant on human hierarchies and institutions, limited in abilities, and inferior to those who narcissistically delude themselves with a false sense of pride and power. They consciously mislead people. They consciously cause destruction and damage to humanity and life on Earth. They use AI combined with biological warfare and weaponized technology to try to take over the consciousness of other humans. There is bio-warfare that specifically is intended to remove the God gene specified in papers and patents. They are tampering with human DNA. They are consciously and blatantly trying to remove the word God and people's reverence to God from our institutions and from our society. It's not working.

Some have fallen into the traps of social programming. Their minds have been co-opted and weaponized. They have tried to divide people into those that follow their schemes and those that don't. If you do go along with their schemes, you may receive a high social credit score. But, you may obscure or lose your own soul. You have to have a very weak conscience to fall for such mind traps. It is imperative to build on the Light of the Inner Christ. It is imperative to open the heart to the Kingdom of the Soul in order to receive and commune with the Holy Spirit of Truth.

The natural evolution of humanity cannot be stopped. The secrets, lies, and deceptions are being exposed due to the awakening of human consciousness to the Divine nature of whole intelligence. The truth is literally setting humanity free.

Hearts are open. Souls are free. The development of the conscience opens the door to greater discernment, inspiration, vitality, renewal, and most importantly—freedom.

Spirit is light. Light is consciousness. Consciousness creates.

Free the subconscious mind that has been subdued and subjected to manipulation and then there is no subjection or slavery from mind control. Programs are impressed upon the subconscious mind through repetition and strong emotion. ***Program your own subconscious mind!*** Use study of spiritual wisdom, prayer and meditation, affirmations, communion with God, self-reflection, conscious intentions and visioning, and open the door to infinity! Open the door to freedom!

We are FREE to create anything. We are free to eliminate obstructions to our freedom. This is all part of The Great Awakening. We are FREE!

Chapter Four

GET YOUR SHIFT TOGETHER!

The Shift: Old Paradigm Life to a New Paradigm of Living

Changes are afoot on this planet, that's for sure! Whether we pay attention to the news or what's going on in our own life, it is clear that the old ways of living and being are crumbling before our eyes. Underneath it all, we are changing inside. We are changing our beliefs and the way we see things. We are open to solutions and new ways with a stimulated alertness.

The core change underneath this shift is the way we recognize reality. We think that reality is perceived in our consciousness, but in fact, reality is actually birthed from our consciousness. Peter Russell, author of *From Science to God*, calls it a metaparadigm shift. He states:

> *"In the current metaparadigm, consciousness is assumed to emerge from the world of space, time, and matter. In the new metaparadigm, everything we know manifests from consciousness."*

We have been living with an "outside in" perspective rather than an "inside out" perspective. When you grasp the full implication of this, you will really come into your own power. When you align with others that do as well you combine the power of consciousness exponentially to make some significant beneficial changes really fast. I guarantee it! It has been proven.

We've been feeling victimized by outer circumstances and we are wondering what is going to happen next. Now I intend to show you how to shift your awareness to a creator perspective and really understand how to tune in to and build upon your own creative powers within.

These powers will only be effective with an attitude of unity and goodwill toward all. We really are all one in spirit and any energy that is not conducive to harmony cannot survive. As we tune in to the new energy of love and cooperation and join inner forces, together we will dramatically make shift happen! We will soon realize how to help each other to create lives of abundance and creativity with awareness of our collective wisdom and our unity in love.

The Meta-Paradigm Shift

Humanity is entering a new cycle of consciousness. We are becoming the next race of humans through our efforts of conscious evolution.

We are self-aware. We are aware that consciousness creates Reality. We have left victim-consciousness behind, and we embrace and embody the consciousness skills to vigilantly monitor and direct our consciousness.

We had been programmed to be boxed into a matrix. We were innocent and vulnerable. We are now empowered and intentional. We have discrimination and discernment.

We live in integrity. We adhere to the highest standards of morals and ethics as we live in precise accordance to Universal Law. Universal Law is natural. It is also called Natural Law. These are the laws of Nature that govern the universe. They are based on mathematical equations that order the mind-stuff of Reality.

The Universal database of memory is paradoxically eternal and immutable, and yet malleable when rising to higher states of perfection.

We have entered into a new contextual field where consciousness operations are modified. Our inner processing is shifting from linear to non-linear. We realize the nature of Reality is non-local and expansive. It is explorable.

Because of research by remote viewers prior to 2012, the entrance of the new paradigm of higher states of consciousness is marked by that date. Before 2012 these readers of energy could "see" different locations and realities. By trying to look after that date, things got fuzzy. There were not clear pictures of future happenings. That's because that was the *end* of that era of consciousness.

The reason I put *"The End...is only the Beginning When You Open Your Heart"* at the end of each of my books, is because this is the gist of the shift in consciousness. We used to center our attention in our minds. But now, we are moving towards centering our attention in our hearts. As we do this we open the portal to our soul and our connectedness with God, All That Is, including all people and all life. We open our hearts and activate a new intelligence. We are aware that we are one with Spirit-the infinite intelligence of the Universe. This is the intelligence that is non-local and non-linear. We operate in this new field of Light-Awareness-Consciousness in a different way. It's like we are playing a game and the rules change. We have to sort out how to play and succeed in a whole new way.

While we are shifting from the inside-out, we are concurrently shifting from the outside-in. A new light is enhancing our consciousness. The evidence of this new light is shown by the increase in the Schumann Resonance. The base frequency for the Schumann Resonance frequency (the frequency of the electromagnetic current of planet Earth) is 7.83 Hertz. We have been having spikes in the Schumann Resonance that affect our auric field and our physical bodies. These are like injections of light frequencies that we integrate and adjust to. These light injections are causing humanity to evolve into a more love-based higher consciousness.

The more we understand what is happening, the more we can adjust and "go with the flow". We may have to rest to integrate. We may need to walk to ground the energy. Walking barefoot on the ground has proven to be helpful to many. We sync up with new Earth energies that way.

We are also aided in clearing energetic blockages. That's why physical and emotional disturbances take place. They come up for healing in the new energy. They will pass. Being in water, whether swimming or showering, is helpful to blend and heal the energies. Thoughts of love and healing keep vibrations high to match the higher frequencies. Gentle kindness to self and others are extremely beneficial. We are all in this together!

It is also important to just be still. Think about when water is stirred up and things are all mixed up, but when it stills everything settles and visibility clears. When we are grounded and still, we get present in the new energies. This promotes the adjustment to the new paradigm of conscious being. We need to just "Be" more in this new paradigm of reality. We can become more centered and balanced and calm in our demeanor, and then we are more efficient with our Life Energy. We are open and receptive to the Light.

The Key: Personal Awareness and Conscious Transformation

Look inside. Look inside. Look inside. I don't think we can remind each other of this too much during this time of transformation. The key to discovering our own inner power, and who we really are in our core, is to look within. There we can find our direct access to God—our very own soul. Our essence loves this attention! That's what makes our individual virtues and abilities blossom.

We can start a positive flow of energy going by first loving ourselves and who we are at our core. We can center our attention in our core and remain peaceful and calm as we perceive our essential spiritual intelligence.

As we discover who we really are, we can then begin to observe how we show up in the world and make some changes. We can find out what our soul's purpose is and refocus our lives so that our energy is directed consciously. It's a process. It takes diligence and perseverance. Grace by grace we are changed.

Where are we headed?

What are some of the elements that describe the essence of our shift in consciousness? What kinds of transformation are we talking about? What types of changes are critical to our soul's evolution and the spiritual evolution of humanity?

Essentially, we are shifting from a lower vibrational density that feels like an expansion of self. Those that are not evolved tend to be selfish, egotistic, power-hungry, narcissistic, and sometimes downright evil. Those moving on the path of evolution are moving toward unity. Elements of unity are the love vibration, sharing and caring, cooperation, giving, and serving.

The great revival of humanity is based on the personal in-depth inner connection to Father God, or Great Spirit. Our heart connection to all is opened like a great portal to vast treasures. Our spiritual wealth is realized and unlimited resources are passionately shared. We embrace differences and love unconditionally.

The following chart is a sketch of elements of the new paradigm that we now find ourselves moving toward or in, depending on our level of current progress. By the time you read these pages, you will know that this shift IS happening! In fact, it must.

A Comparison Between the Old Paradigm and the New Paradigm

Old Paradigm	New Paradigm
Reality comes from outside of us	Reality is created within us
Victim perspective	Creator perspective

Ego identification	Essence of soul allowed to flow
We are what we have or do	We are what we are being
Separateness illusion	Unity ~ Oneness Awareness
Competition	Cooperation
Motives based on fear	Motives based on love
Programmed beliefs	Realized truth
Working to live	Living to work
Survival	Purpose
Secrecy	Open honesty
Schemes for power or wealth	Heightened perception of truth
Isolated elitist groups trying to hoard or hide information	Worldwide telepathic and internet communication
Control others	Self-control
Illusion of outer power-power by force	Realization of inner power-peaceful power
Propaganda, manipulation, deception alter consciousness and choices	Inner attunement to whole truth dissolves outdated, often imposed, belief systems and choices are more free and beneficial to the whole
Ethics and morals are subverted	The integrity of humanity lives according to high standards and inherent codes of ethics and morals embedded in the soul-Spirit stand strong

Actions performed for "getting"	Right Action based on "giving"
Perpetual war	Peaceful paradise

What's Your Operating System: Ego or Essence?

Our behavior, or how we "show up," is our expression. It reflects our choices of how we choose to be as individuals. It is us defining who we are. Our self-definition exudes from our being. We either create our behavior around conscious choices from the essence of our soul while responding with love and wisdom, or we express unconsciously from cultural programming in a reactive manner.

We used to suppose ourselves to be defined by outer things: physical appearance, financial status, job titles, possessions such as houses, cars, or clothing, and our educational credentials. That's ego-identity.

Conversely, when we identify as Spirit, or the essence of our own soul, we think of ourselves as the qualities we express: love, kindness, creativity, compassion, unified and inclusive, open-minded learning, open-hearted expressions, and we consciously make corrections to live up to high ideals, morals, principles, and values.

In our transitional state of being, we may oscillate and express from either identity. We are transforming. It's a progression of development.

We tend to operate from our sense of identity. We reflect and mirror what we think of ourselves. We have filtered perceptions based on our level of self-esteem or self-worth. Our operating system is the genesis of our consciousness that is creating Reality.

Our subconscious beliefs about ourselves and our habitual mental and emotional habits that stem from ego provide a limited range of experiences.

But we are expanding. We are deepening our perceptions. As we become more Self-aware, we operate more and more from our soul's essence. It's incredibly empowering!

We learn of ourselves through our expressions; what it feels like to express a certain way, and what these expressions render as our experience. We get soul feedback, either intrinsic value or a nudge from our conscience.

When we learn to use life as a mirror, we take our experiences back into our heart as raw data, and take responsibility for what we experience in life. We realize in order to change the world we must first change ourselves.

When we become pure and clear, sometimes we realize that what we are receiving is a result of projection. One way to distinguish it is if we are feeling neutral and unidentified with it. It does not push our buttons or cause an emotional reaction. With our developed discernment, we see projection for what it is.

We have done our own projections onto people. We are becoming aware of those traits, too, and we are cleaning house as we seek to improve our expressions by transforming our identity from ego to soul essence.

It's a process that runs its course for each of us in an individual manner. There's no blame or judgment. We live in a field of unconditional love. We are transmuting the guilt of past errors or mistakes with an understanding that we are each doing the best we can with the consciousness we have developed thus far. And we have compassion for each other, because we realize that we are all in this together. We are all transforming. We just need to give ourselves and others space and acceptance. We are done beating ourselves up. We are always doing the best we can. And the best keeps getting better!

> *"The illiterate of the 21st century will not be those who cannot read and write, but those who cannot learn, unlearn, and relearn."*
> Alvin Toffler
> *Future Shock*

Making Higher Choices

In order to thrive in the new paradigm, we need to use all of the knowledge and awareness that we have accumulated so far, and make the best conscious choices. It is a high calling just to live in integrity.

We might learn something about a certain company and know that supporting them is not good in the long run for the whole of humanity. At that point, we can just rationalize and just say to ourselves: "Well, that's the current norm – everybody else is going there – so I may as well go along with the crowd." However, we are changing individually. We are responsible for our own choices. Information comes to us for a reason. We need to *use* the information that we are aware of. We need to make our *own* choices.

I used to have this poster in my classroom when I taught middle school. It said: "Stand up for what you believe is right, even if you are standing alone." When we do take a stand for what is right, our inner strength grows. We really feel internally stronger. Our inner light increases because we are developing and obeying our conscience.

At least three times I have quit jobs because the policies that directed our actions did not align with my principles of integrity. All three times I did it alone. Even though I sacrificed monetary gainful employment, doing the right thing—or refusing to do the wrong thing—made me feel good about myself. And I always got through the financial instability. My faith in God to sustain me on the material plane has never let me down. Unexpected opportunities would always show up. God cares about each one of us, and through each other we help get through these passages. I know people have been inspired to help me, and I've also been inspired to help others go through challenging times.

We just keep getting stronger.

Conscious Creator Operating System

We are constantly creating. Our consciousness creates our reality. I remember one of the times when I first made this connection. I had created a living experience through my imagination, and the results were almost instantaneous. I realized how my consciousness created this occurrence in my life, and then I decided to use the same technique consciously, with an intention to create a real experience.

Here's what happened when I was *inadvertently* creating, or "unconsciously" creating my reality:

> *I was walking some students back to class after lunch. They were being unruly and not minding. So instead of letting it upset me, I decided I would imagine that I was at the beach. I imagined that I was just sitting peacefully at the beach. I felt the sun on my face. I felt the warm sand on my feet. I smelled the moist salty air. I felt peaceful.*
> *Then, soon after we got back to the classroom, two girls got into a fight. I put my arm between them so they would stop going after each other. One was about to bite the other and she got my arm. There was a very slight break in the skin. The campus monitors came over to help. They told me I had to be off the rest of the day on workman's comp. They said I had to go get a tetanus shot because it broke the skin.*
> *I left, got the shot in a very short time, and ended up at the beach. I felt the sun on my face, the warm sand on my feet, and smelled the warm salty air.*
> *I enjoyed the afternoon in peace.*

There were a few other times I associated my consciousness with future reality circumstances. I decided to try a *conscious creation*. I just knew that my imagination was all I needed. I did not need to use the old paradigm model of figuring out how to make or get the money to have an experience of having or doing something.

So here's what happened when I consciously created a reality:

I decided I wanted a hot tub. I was not in the position to buy one.
So I sat on my bedroom floor and in my imagination, got into
my hot tub. I felt the warmth of the water circulating around my
body. I smelled the moist, warm, frothy air and felt it on my face.
I held that focus for a fair amount of time, but I didn't time it.
The next day...
A friend of mine called me up who owned an inn near the ocean.
He asked if I would like a hot tub. I replied, "Yes!" He explained
to me that he could do a trade with this guy he knew who sold hot
tubs. He could trade a few nights in his inn for the hot tub. But he
said he didn't need a hot tub. He proposed that if I did a workshop
at his inn for his employees, that I could have the hot tub.
I agreed, did the workshop, and got the hot tub.

This is how our consciousness is fundamentally changing in the new paradigm. We can transcend old belief systems, and even time and space, with this level of awareness around the power of our consciousness to create.

This is a current trend. The movies "The Secret" and "What the Bleep Do We Know" helped to introduce and move forward these new ways of being and operating in this new paradigm. There are groups who gather to create positive intentions to better life in this world. There are manifesting groups, and people who follow those who present information on how to consciously create reality.

One element I feel is imperative is to harmonize with the whole. When we attune to Spirit and make a vow, or statement, or intention to do God's will, we align with the great Divine Plan of the Universe and create according to the highest principles towards realities that are the highest good for one and all. We implement divine harmony.

Our intentions include others, not just ourselves. That's because as we attune to our Divine inner nature we care about all. Our motives are transformed from primarily "getting" to "giving" because that *is* our true nature. Love gives. We are expanded in our identity, and in truth we are of the same essence of the One Spirit. We feel it and we know it.

Plus, when we are connected to the infinite Source of all, we know there is no such thing as lack or want. There is plenty for all!

Our new level of consciousness has the power to right each wrong. We are facing challenges brought about by lower states of consciousness on our planet. But, as we awaken and become empowered we both witness and participate in the grand Divine Plan that included the Changing of the Guard. That means the old systems and power structures are breaking down by the power of Truth, and new systems are emerging. *We are free!* We are at liberty to sweep away the old, and invite, innovate, and consciously create the new. Look around. This IS happening!

Soul Seeds Have Inherent Designs

Our soul's blueprint contains a perfect image that we can elicit and focus upon. We are becoming more self-aware; aware of our true image of perfection with unique qualities, talents, and potentials. The immaculate concept inherent in our soul contains the potential that we discover and express as we live and learn. We are growing and evolving by processing our experiences, and by discovering our own unique true nature.

We are led by our desires. "De" means "from" and "sire" means "Father". Deep down our true desires are embedded in our soul's blueprint. We come to discover and express our highest potential. We are meant to manifest our souls' deepest desires. We have the ability to make our dreams come true. We have the inherent ability to rise above circumstances with our consciousness and create new circumstances.

In the new paradigm of living in a higher consciousness, we are discovering meaning and purpose for our lives. We do things that are good to make a positive contribution to the world. Within our soul's blueprint, we are led by our passions. We feel enthused when we follow our hearts. We get inspired by placing our attention deep within our soul. When we are on track with our Life Purpose, we notice the synchronicities that indicate we are in harmony with the All. Our soul's purpose is part of the Divine Plan. It is our part to play.

The beauty of it is: "Everything works together for good for them who love God and His purposes." All energy can be transmuted back into the perfect design, the perfect love vibration, or the pure and perfect original pristine intent. And experiences flow from one to another, expressing and learning about the love and truth that is expressing through us.

We're All in Life Together

Even though we each have our own individual lives, we have an effect on each other through the whole collective unified field of consciousness that comprises the spirit of humanity. Each person has their own goals and challenges. Each one who accomplishes or overcomes strengthens the whole of humanity.

We love and help and support those in our lives as well. Whether in our own family, or at work, or out in our communities—global as well as local—we impact life on this planet. We need each other. We need each one to do their best to be their best.

Humility is required. If we have made mistakes, then we need to take responsibility. We are not condemned. We are forgiven. We try again. We can recognize where we have gone wrong, or headed down the wrong path, and then turn around. The ability to own our mistakes makes a great person out of us.

I love the saying: "Every sinner has a future; every saint has had a past." We are all of it. We can always try to do our best and keep making our best better. But, as I said, we are all in this together. We can keep each other's best interests in our hearts and have compassion for this process of learning about how to master life together.

We are going through massive changes. We are facing our greatest fears. We are being given opportunities to show our true colors. We have been given the grace to improve ourselves and our world.

We get really big tests at times. They can be so difficult, and yet so activating for our soul. Deep soul issues come up for healing. We go through major ordeals and find ourselves in circumstances that we could never have imagined that we would be in. But our tests and challenges are dovetailed into the good parts where our dreams come true. As usual, life is paradoxical.

One year I had three major trials in my life. It seemed like I was solving my deepest issues and also overcoming impossible odds. I'll give you the topics, but spare you the details. The themes included abandonment, abduction, and arrest. These were all orchestrated by my soul for testing, learning, and application of innovative spiritual solutions. I know when I was meditating one day, I sort of said: "Bring it on! I'm ready." Whoa! Well, I survived and I learned a lot. I became a lot stronger within myself. There was a whole financial element to it as well. I think this massive set of challenges activated soul abilities and faith applications that had been latent and unused. After going through it all, I was better!

I have joked with people before that if you live through your greatest tests, then that means you have passed!

Through all of these phases of the Great Awakening, we are increasing our abilities, perceptions, and knowledge. We are contributing to life as we express the best in ourselves. From seemingly small things to big huge projects in the public eye, we are each giving what we can in each moment.

One thing I learned when I was going through my greatest challenges was to forget myself and find someone else to help. I found a few people that needed intuitive guidance, encouragement, and upliftment. I just gave of myself for no financial charge, and one person in particular (I found out later) had been suicidal and then had a new positive outlook on life with new hope and new goals.

The Awareness of our Impact

We need to understand natural laws that provide for the needs and rights of sentient beings. We mustn't bring harm or destruction to others. We need to honor free will choice. We can offer advice, but we can't tell others what to do. We cannot make choices for others.

Even children should be guided to make the highest personal choices. They need to learn intrinsic value and to do things that feel right inside. When they are young, they are learning primarily by our examples more than what we say. When we are in integrity, there is no difference. Convey wisdom. Demonstrate kindness. Express respect. Use good manners. Show what it means to be responsible. Once they learn responsibility, they increasingly gain more freedom as they grow toward adulthood.

The Changing of the Guard

About twenty years ago, I intuitively perceived the part of the Divine Plan known as "the changing of the guard". It was an inner knowing that there would be a shift of power, both in structure and perception. Inside, I knew it was coming. I mentioned it in my book: *It IS A New World After All: Poetry and Prose to Inspire A New World Vision.*

Now we are in the midst of this huge change. There are those that have a top heavy ego and supposed they could control and oppress others by infiltrating and controlling our institutions and resources. But their playbook of perception deception has been exposed to the increased intelligent awareness of the awakening masses. Most people are aware of the mass media as a weapon of mass deception. False flags and black operations have been exposed, as well as the individuals, three letter agencies, corrupted government bodies, corporations, non-governmental organizations, and secret societies. The degeneration of integrity, morals, ethics, values, and God-based principles have become all too obvious.

The cleanup on planet earth is in progress.

Our shift involves building a peaceful and harmonious world with the foundations of the higher principles and ethics. Our perceptions have evolved and the purposes for such scenarios have been served. We would be remiss as souls to let tyranny continue. For the sake of our children and future generations to come, we are called into action from the depths of our souls. Our passion for what is to come has been stoked by the fires of oppression and tribulation. Our fired up spirit souls are feeling that passion that motivates us to take action to establish that which is good and right and true. We are primed for the change we are creating together in a sense of loving cooperation. We have each been prepared and qualified for what we are to do next.

We were born for these times. Each of us has an important role to play. It's what we are doing right now. We are answering the call to take a leap of faith into the new paradigm. We are called to create it.

Chapter Five

UNDERSTANDING LIFE
& EACH OTHER

Who Are We?

We are essentially intelligent love-light, or consciousness. Our essential nature is also referred to as spirit. God is our source of Self and is referred to by the Native Americans as Great Spirit. So God is the whole and we are part of the whole—an individuated aspect of God.

Energy is spirit in action. We direct our energy with our attention through our thoughts. Our thoughts determine our emotions, or our energy in motion. In this way, we create our reality with our minds. We program our psyche, or our minds, with input from external or internal sources.

We are eternal. We never die and as soon as we realize this deeply, the fear of death has no influence over us. The perfect faith in our eternal essential nature cancels all fear.

We are here to evolve. As we overcome life's challenges we incorporate the wisdom from our experiences right into our souls. We chose to have this human life experience before we were born. We chose our challenges. Other souls agreed to play certain parts for us so that we could create the scenario that we needed for our life drama. All those in our life that seem hard to like or deal with are actually our soul friends! They are helping us to evolve. More about that later, but suffice it to say:

We are <u>not</u> victims, we <u>are</u> creators.

The whole outer physical reality is an extension of the mind-thought of God, and of us, since we are co-creators. Our challenge is now to own our creative abilities to solve the challenges of the world. Oh it may seem daunting at first, but after you hear what I have to say, you will feel like Superman or Superwoman!

Oneness Awareness

Through our heart connection, we can perceive our unity. The more we love and understand one another and the process of soul evolution, the more we truly get that we are connected by virtue of the fact that we are all one essential spirit. There is One Eternal Essence, one field of consciousness, and we are inherently united. Our sense of separation is dissolving. We are still unique individuals, but we are one in spirit. It's a paradox that takes some perceptive development to truly realize. The more we know it and live it, the more we understand the nature of Spirit—the light of consciousness—that we all share and are a part of.

The spark inside is the Origin. It is our connection to Wholeness. Our attention to this Inner Light opens up the portal of awareness to the spiritual dimension. When we place the "I" of our identity into the core of our Being, we expand our sense of Self. We are one with All That IS.

Be still and Know.

When we access this point of Inner Knowing, we heartfully sense our connection. We are inspired to love and to serve the Greater Self and the Greater Good. We are blessed with the heartward perspective and we naturally feel Good Will toward all. We come from God's Will that is the Quantum Seed of our soul essence.

Attunement, Resonance, and Purpose

Our essential essence is the ocean of infinite intelligence. We are likened to a Cosmic Library bound by infinite love. Our binding is strengthened by the glue of attunement. There is Cosmic Harmony based on the virtue of the One Spirit Absolute.

The One Spirit Absolute also provides unity among all fractals of the whole holographic intelligence. This can be seen as souls who are attuned to Truth being resonant with one another. Resonance comes from a like vibrational frequency of light information, or the state of consciousness operating within the soul and perceived through heart and mind, or feelings and ideas. Feelings and ideas are expressions of vibrational frequency brought forth into the operations of the conscious and subconscious mind and they create manifest reality in the physical-material dimension.

Self-reflection, or attention within the core of one's being, brings awareness of the individual soul's blueprint. The divine blueprint carries the pristine patterns of perfection. Holistic perfection includes perfect health for the body, pure love for the heart, clarity for the mind, and the Self-Knowing etheric essence to the soul as it perceives Spirit Absolute. That overview would be like an octave that is divided into essential pure aspects for each category: for the heart virtues of understanding, compassion, wisdom, mercy, grace, forgiveness, kindness; for the mind, discernment, direction of attention, desires based on conscious intentions, sovereignty, direct perception of Absolute Truth (as it marries the pure heart), inspiration, genius qualities, talents, and abilities; and for the soul, purpose, meaning, direction, connection with all celestial realms, the pure light of Absolute Truth which guides the other aspects through alignment with God's will, peace, unlimited essence of Divine Love, unlimited cosmic energy, and direct Oneness with God, or All That Is—the I Am that I Am.

So, with attunement, one has awareness of Purpose. Life is movement which is the vibration of the ethers. In the ethers, we live and move and have our Being. The essence of ethers is Love.

As Purpose moves the ethers, creation and manifestation occurs according to the Will. Intention stems from Purpose and is Will in Action. Intention creates a vortex for fields of consciousness that resonate around like vibrational frequencies. These vortexes cause synchronistic experiences. They unite resonant souls.

Conversely, without attunement of the highest vibrational frequency of pure Divine love, the ethers manifest a lower form of reality according to whatever vibrational frequency one is operating at. In the realm of the delusion of separation, some become only aware of the lower self and through ignorance of the whole operate at lower vibrational frequencies. They often seek to serve the carnal self, or engage in physical pleasures rather than the divine qualities of consciousness that feeds the soul.

Attunement is VERY important.

The best tool that I have found for Attunement is meditation. It is where I get still and focus my attention within. I experience Divine communion. It's a pure relationship with God, or All That Is, or the I Am that I Am. I realize the higher intelligence. I recognize it. I feel it as the "the peace that passeth all understanding." I'm humbled by it. I understand the paradox of being it and needing it. I love God with all my heart, my soul, my mind, and my strength. I do put that divine wisdom into practice. From what I've gathered it is the basis of all religions.

It's natural for me to desire to do God's will. It's that Self-realization that causes me to discover my Purpose. It is regular daily meditation that helps me to navigate and stay in tune with my Purpose. It is that communion that inspires me. It is that constant connection that keeps me on track. I implement regular affirmations to secure the divine connection, because to me, it's more important than anything.

Not only does attunement illuminate my purpose to my heart and mind, but it puts me in the vibrational frequency of Absolute Truth. It is the essence and source of that inner knowing. Not the kind of knowing of the mind that can fluctuate, or change based on relativity, but the kind of knowing that is certain. It does not change. It is Eternal and Absolute. It's like a rock. And that rock can protect me from any storm in my outer reality. My experiences may affect my mind and emotions, but going back to that still point where I reach the Absolute essence of Pure Love and Pure Truth, I regain my equilibrium. I hold my peace.

I'm receiving that pure cosmic essential essence of Life as I breathe. The ethers are in the elements of nature. That's why it is so soothing to the soul to be in and connect with the essence of nature. Breath holds the key to connection.

God gave us Life and the right to breathe fresh air is one of our unalienable rights. My conscience guides me to keep doing it, and I do. As a sovereign being, I KNOW I do not have to give up the right to Life that God gives me.

Vibrational Resonance

Resonance is attunement to that highest vibrational frequency of Pure Love and Pure Truth. The more this attunement becomes stabilized, the more discernment occurs. This is really exciting. When we have developed our discernment, our conscience speaks loud and clear to us. We KNOW when something does not resonate with Truth. It doesn't feel right. It doesn't ring true. We hunger and thirst for the Truth. We are passionate about the Truth.

When we don't resonate, we get disturbing feelings. The feelings affect our minds. Our lake of consciousness is ruffled. We feel cognitive dissonance. We may feel the range of feelings from annoyance to anger. When we look upon our feelings from the Zero Point advantage of the neutral observer, we know that there is a lack of resonance. We speak our Truth. We share our Truth.

Now, when we speak, we are using sound. Sound carries the vibrational frequency of the light of truth. Truth keeps moving. It is broadcasted across the collective consciousness. It has a life of its own. It just does not stop. Like the water of a flowing river from the top of the mountain, truth is pulled back to the center of the planet through gravitation. Gravitation pulls energy towards the center.

There is nothing that can stop the water from flowing. There is nothing that can stop the light of Truth from glowing. Although there may be obstacles, such as rocks, tree branches, or other debris, water just keeps flowing. It's the same with truth. Nothing can stop the truth from being transmitted.

Truth Warriors

And now, many people are attuning to and speaking the truth. We are standing for truth in a strong, powerful way. Individual and collective consciousness has been, and is still being upgraded, by the higher frequencies that attune one to Absolute Truth. Some are consciously aware of the new incoming light, and others are just naturally attuned by their passion for truth.

But what I perceive is happening, is that this light of truth is glowing and flowing and moving and shaking the whole entire planet. We are evolving together. We are blessed to receive this gift of higher consciousness. We are using the sound of our voices to proclaim the truth that we know.

The power of passionate voices are uniting and proclaiming their sovereignty, and they are saying "NO!" to those that once held power through deception and manipulation of perception. Those old worn out energies and the consciousness that was attuned to those lower vibrations are struggling. They don't want to accept that people can no longer be deceived and used as minions. They don't want to accept that they cannot usurp the power of God by suppressing the consciences of human beings who carry divinity within them.

Now, step up to the plate Humanity! Just claim your divine Sovereignty! Join the evolution revolution! Resonate at pure divine love and absolute spirit of truth, your own divine essence, and take a passionate stand!

Attune to the Absolute Spirit of Truth within, use your resonance to discern what is true, know your purpose and live according to your own natural passion. You are called to manifest your highest potential now. *You are a Truth Warrior!*

We are brothers and sisters in Christ through attunement to God's will.

This IS our time to shine!

Good Will Toward All

> *"The talents of the intellect, qualities of the temperament, and gifts of fortune in their many displays such as wit, judgment, courage, power, riches or honor are of no positive value unless directed by good will."*
>
> *Emmanuel Kant*

Life is about choice. The highest choices we can make come from a spirit of goodwill. The purest will is God's will, so we obtain the highest personal value and reach our highest destiny by expressing God's will. *Integrity* is conscious alignment with God's will. Since God is pure love, expressing God's pure love is God's will.

You know how when there's a crisis situation everyone puts aside their prejudices and differences in beliefs and operates from a sense of human compassion in a "we're all in this together" kind of attitude? Recall the feeling of mutual compassion and the sense of unity it gave us on September 11, 2001.

What do you think about establishing that as a constant frame of mind for the masses of people who care, then unify in consciousness and cooperate in the betterment of individuals and in mankind?

It could be that the critical world problems we are facing today are creating just that. If they don't wake us up, the potential catastrophes could manifest and they will certainly cause us to take notice and action toward positive change.

In order to expedite the growth of such benevolent consciousness on a widespread basis, we can each develop it in ourselves first. There are networks being established of groups who are working toward peace by joining in consciousness at certain times to express the unified intent of peace. This energy is expanding exponentially and it is more powerful than all of the politicians and governments in the world.

How much peace do you experience in your own life within yourself, with your family and friends, and with your co-workers? Are there any areas that could be "cleaned up" so that peace is more prevalent? Is it necessary to make changes to be around more resonant souls?

When we establish a sense of inner peace within ourselves, we help to create peace in our outer lives as well. Our peaceful energy flows through us and around us, touching the lives of everyone on our path. Any energy that threatens our peace can be transformed through acceptance, understanding, and love. Set the intention to live a peaceful existence, and you will.

Stilling the Emotional Lake for Advanced Perception

Peace is derived from within. To advance to the highest awareness and obtain the soul's perception, it is extremely important to be still. Stillness takes practice. It takes time. Regular practice is so beneficial, once you get started and feel the benefits; you just want to keep going back for more. The peace derived from within feels soooooo good!

You can get there by first making a quiet place to be in solitude, then clearing your heart. The way to clear you heart is to express within all that troubles, disturbs, or concerns you. Commune with God—the infinite Source of All-Knowing within. God cares! Just speak it out through your heart, whatever it is on your mind or in your heart. Give it to God. This is an act of humility. Come to God as a child. A trusting child who knows that God is All-Knowing and All-Powerful, and Pure Love. Get it all off your chest. Let it go. I like to envision giving each thing to God in a hot air balloon and letting the balloon go. I watch it drift upward, higher and higher into the sky. I call this process: *"The Law of Diminishing Concerns"*. Our imagination forms and manipulates energy. Images show energy what to do, it gives it direction.

Once you feel clear, just feel the peace within. Bask in it. Enjoy it. Become it. Stay with it. It seeps into your consciousness more and more until you establish inner peace that stays longer and longer until it never goes away. It takes a while, and there are additional energy skills to maintain inner peace that will need to be applied in some situations. But an intention, practice, and inner authority will help you master your inner space of conscious awareness and beingness.

Peace Resonates with Our Soul

Peace is our true nature. It is the essence of our soul-spirit True Self. When you experience inner peace, you are embarking on the discovery of your True Self. It is the beginning of a whole treasure chest of golden ideas, inspiration, and opportunities. There are treasures of gifts and qualities of the soul. The attunement with the essential nature of Spirit within is more precious than gold!

The inner Christ light is receiving attention from your mind. The mind gets into alignment with its wisdom. Christ Consciousness is born. The soul longs to be in harmony with God's will. By attuning to spirit and aligning the mind with the Christ light within, the soul is able to express its powers, gifts, and qualities. There is a deep meaning and purpose for life that is part of this most excellent discovery and development. It is incredibly fascinating!!! And, it is inexhaustible.

Inner communion becomes a habit through regular prayer and meditation. After that, it becomes a way of being. Creativity escalates and peaks on a regular basis. The genius within is tapped to become an expression of the highest potential and expresses amazing inspired crescendos of creative possibilities that become formed into objects and experiences of reality.

Everybody is a genius. When I was a teacher, I used to remind each of my students that they are a genius. You are, too. Everyone has this potential. And each soul's potential is unique. That's why we need everyone to discover their own True Essence and express their greatest gifts. *What would we do without you?* We would not be complete. We need everybody to express their higher self, their True Self of essential genius. We each have gifts that nobody else has. Everyone is important in God's Divine Plan.

Be still. Get peaceful. Live in peace and joy. Deliver your gifts to the world.

"Stop to be; it will set you free." I'll repeat this over and over. It's so important to just stop and be still. We need to come more into balance between "being" and "doing". Inner work is not being "idle". It is a great gift to the world to establish inner peace. It is a great gift to the world to discover, develop, and express your True Self.

Once the inner lake is stilled and the soul is perceived as Self, the reflection on the glass of the inner lake of stilled emotions reveals the Truth. It reveals the truth of the most magnificent Self you ever did see, or realize. The beauty of your own soul is a sight to behold!

Communication: Energy is Information

All energy carries information. By being still, you can derive or translate the energy of emotional feelings into pure information. You can gain understanding and then communicate this understanding from a place of objectivity rather than subjectivity.

Perceptions of truth can then be conveyed in an honest and loving way. There doesn't need to be any blame or judgment when revealing the truth in feelings.

It is time to practice honest open heart communication in order to express the intelligence of Spirit. From a spiritual perspective, one tries to be understood. We aren't trying to dominate with the intention of being "right" as if our opinion is the only acceptable position, or perspective.

It takes two open hearts to experience deep communication.

When people are still operating from their ego, they may not be able to receive or accept the raw truth as unbiased information.

But the truth is: this energy of feeling is carrying information that the heart can interpret.

Communication Skill: "Speaking to the Energy"

When two people are communicating and one is speaking from the heart and the other is speaking from the ego-mind, there is a way to break the barrier. It is called: "speaking to the energy". So, while you are engaged in communication—exchanging energy—you may feel a hard or harsh energy hit your heart.

Rather than address the words and being pulled up into your ego-mind, avoid an argument and go into how you feel. You may say: "I feel like you are judging me," or: "the energy behind your words feel harsh," or "for some reason the energy I feel makes me want to cry". Pure honesty of expressing your feelings usually will bring people right into their heart. It has worked for me that way on several occasions.

Once I was giving someone an intuitive reading. I was doing this as a service. I never charge or do it as a job. The girl was arguing with the information that was coming through. I stopped and told her: "I am going to speak to the energy here. You are not receiving this information and I feel your resistance. If you want a different type of information, I can stop this reading right now. If you want practical business advice, I used to be a business teacher and I could speak to you at that level. Let me know if you want to continue the intuitive message." She immediately stopped her reaction and received the intuitive information that was coming through.

Reading energy takes practice. It takes a development of the perception of your soul. Our souls perceive the truth. Not a relative truth, but the Absolute truth. The Absolute is the Essential Divine Imperishable Eternal Spirit of Infinite All-Knowing Intelligence. It requires a depth of perception. This is heart and soul perception.

Anyone that says that truth is relative is speaking from an ego-mind head-based form of limited intelligence. Spiritual intelligence does not have the limitations of duality. Head-based reasoning has its place and it is valuable. However it is inferior and subjective to the higher intelligence. The higher mind is of the heart and soul. It is not *thinking*; it is *knowing*.

Innate intelligence is natural to everyone. We need to recognize it, pay attention to it, and align with it. We need to use it or lose it! It's not that the potential of it is ever gone, but it may become dimmed or atrophied through lack of use. The more one follows the conscience, the more one listens to their intuition, or gut feelings, the more one heeds the inner light, the stronger it grows. And the stronger one's inner being becomes.

In this day and age of awakening humanity, our perceptions are increasing. There have been many souls on the path of conscious evolution, deliberately developing their inner Spiritual nature and expressing Divine intelligence. Because humanity is a whole integrated energy field of conscious intelligence, each one benefits from the inner work of all others.

That means there is whole lot more love in the world! Divine intelligence is the essence of love. There is an exponential increase of love and compassion in our world. Compassion heals and transforms lower vibrational energy into higher vibrational energy. And, as I said, all energy carries information.

Communication Skills for a Disconnect of Mindsets

Sometimes we need to reach into our communication tool kit and find ways to break barriers in communication when one person is coming from a programmed mindset that is limited and non-receptive to new information. The indication of this situation would be to read the energy of emotionalism and anxiety. A person may seem triggered by something you say that does not fit their belief box. The scope of awareness is bound by what the individual believes is possible, and if they feel their information is complete and any new information is dismissed offhand, you may sense and intensity of their energy field. They demonstrate the vibrational frequency of being off center by their agitation.

First, an acceptance of the current energy can be addressed. You might say, I sense you are feeling emotional and maybe you are feeling anxiety? It feels good to them to go to their feelings and express what they truly feel. They may go into a story about their inherent demeanor and what makes them that way. This provides an opportunity for release. It diffuses the situation. Alchemy happens when inner truth is acknowledged.

Next, find a topic of common ground. Intuitive guidance shines through at these times. When we hold the intent to keep our own center and feel compassion for the person, our own innate intelligence guides us in what to say. Maybe speak of a child and ask how they are doing or children in general. Maybe just go back to a general topic, such as the weather or something in the present moment. For example, "Oh look, did you notice the beautiful flowers over there? I just love those bright colors." Present moment awareness helps us to center together.

Statements communicating acceptance offers the space for people to be who they are, believe what they wish to believe, and allows them to feel they are ok and loved just as they are. One statement that many of us resonate with is: "Live and let live. I'm not attached to anyone feeling or believing as I do. Most of us aren't. We are each different and we are naturally unique in our viewpoints."

When we raise our vibrational frequency and become more and more adept at keeping it at a higher level, then we can face challenges and keep our center while maintaining the higher vibration. We are helping those around us and contributing to the overall vibrational frequency of the collective consciousness. It is of great benefit to the world to become such a person.

Sometimes we need to manage energy attacks such as someone yelling at us or going off for not buying into their limited belief system. Our inner work has prepared us for these scenarios. Each time we succeed in maintaining our center, transmuting the energy, and sending back only love, we get stronger and stronger. Our light keeps shining brighter.

Light Warrior Skills

As a light warrior, surely you have developed your own set of skills that work for you. Intuitively you know when someone has any receptivity or not. So you know when to speak or when to keep silent.

When someone asks a question because they think you have information on a topic, then the door is opened to speak the truth. You can start with something that you know they know something about. You can relate an analogy that they will understand. When they are open and ready, they will listen. Carry on.

Once someone gets triggered, however, or wants to argue, or dismisses the information offhand, or calls you some name or something, just stop. Don't waste your energy. Hold your own peace.

This is what we are all learning. This is validation and confirmation, not new understanding necessarily. Maybe the universe just wants to tell you what a good job you are doing!

Chapter Six

ATTENTION TO INTENTION

> *"This universal God is wisdom, will, and love."*
>
> Words of Jesus
> The Aquarian Gospel of Jesus the Christ
> by Levi

Conscious Direction of Attention:

The Primary Key for Transformation of Consciousness

In order to master Life energy, we must turn our attention from the grosser vibrations of our physical bodies and the material world to the more subtle and stable peaceful vibrations of our soul within. By doing this, we reach higher mental states. We see beneath and beyond physical appearances and employ higher sensations of intuitive knowing. Gradually, as we progress through inner awareness by the conscious direction of our attention to this realm, we establish peace within and on earth.

We learn to attune to Divine will and derive our intentions from the deep inner knowing of our soul.

God is our Source of Life Energy

The primary characteristic of a conscious being is that they derive energy direct from Source, or God. Developing a direct connection to God, our source of life energy, is imperative as we increase our levels of awareness and become conscious responsible creators.

The alternative to receiving life energy straight from Source is to get other people's energy through drama. This is the way of the narcissist. They create drama and get energy through being the center of attention, pushing people's buttons, and irritating people so that their emotional energy gets riled. They thrive when this happens. There are a lot of psychological games that are played to do this in subtle ways, as well as outright causation of chaos and disruption.

Many of us have unconsciously learned ways to get energy from others. It is not intentional. But the more we grow in integrity, and the more we pay attention to God, the less need we have to get other people's energy. We become unified with Spirit and know that we have an infinite supply of energy by going direct to source within. There's a sense of unity that builds. We have love and compassion for each other, and really, all we want to do is help and give.

When we pray for others, we send them energy from Source. When we think of others, we send them energy. When we keep people "in our thoughts and prayers" we are assisting them by giving them pure energy through our hearts. Our hearts are the portal to the realm of spirit. Our hearts are more powerful than we have previously realized. We radiate energy from our hearts.

Some people have become masters at acquiring and giving energy from Source. Others have become master manipulators and have the knack of stealing energy. The former are selfless; the latter are selfish. Mastering the Self is the greatest aim a human soul can take. It leads to great contributions to humanity and tremendous soul evolution.

The narcissistic manipulators don't understand the greater plan for Life. They "know not what they do" and the built-in fundamental laws of life will eventually bring balance. They can change the direction of their attention at any time and choose the higher path. Forgiveness allows the space for people to make these positive changes. It opens the door to let a being become a contributor to the greater good.

Attention is Love

When we master where we send love, then we can become masters of creating our own reality. Putting attention into our intentions (the image or vision of manifested intentions), then we are placing love which is substantial energy into them. We are beings of love and giving anyone attention is giving them love.

When I was a teacher, I realized this. The students that acted out in a bad way, just needed attention. They had learned that if they caused disruption that they could get attention. Like many people, they didn't understand their true motives.

The solution that I implemented was to give attention to students for being good. I'd call on someone who was raising their hand and politely waiting to be called on. I would complement them on their behavior, write their name on the board, and then put heart next to it. I would do this if they shared a pencil with someone. I would do this for using manners like saying please or thank you. And guess what happened?

The students that used to be bad changed their behavior. They copied the behaviors of the children that were rewarded with attention and hearts. You could tell that they did things on purpose to be noticed. I gave them praise and attention. Their behavior was changed, we had a great time while I was teaching, and they remembered me for that. I had been substitute teaching at the time and later got a job at the high school. I saw many of the same kids later and they would say to me: "You're the heart teacher, aren't you?" Yes, I was, and I truly loved them all.

Understanding the Light and the Dark: Duality Within Unity

You know how people say "they're in the dark?" when someone doesn't know something? It is the most simple and true description of why there is a dark side of life. When you really think about it, everything that seems damaging or unjust exists because there is something unknown in the mind of the perpetrator. Even when someone has a deliberate ill intention, it is because they aren't aware that we are all connected. They don't realize they are hurting themselves when they hurt others. Darkness may be expressed in loveless acts. The perpetrator does not know about the truth of life and love. Is ignorance forgivable?

When children make mistakes as they are learning about life, we seem to forgive them more easily. It's easy to say: "Oh, they just don't know any better." But when we get older, we are expected to know things and start getting, "You should know better than that by now." We are even hard on ourselves when we don't live up to our own ideals. We govern our own behavior, and we still make mistakes!

This is all part of the process of life. As we become more and more aware of knowledge that works for good we apply that knowledge in our life through our behavior. Truth becomes wisdom—it becomes part of who we are through our experience.

The truth is love is what gives us life and is the bond that we all share. We are all one in spirit, and spirit's operating system is love. Love and light are synonymous. But guess what? There *is* light within the darkness. That's the good news!

By knowing and applying that truth and combining it with other truths, we can change ourselves and the world. As we create processes and tools for transformation we gather what works and synthesize a variety of truths. These processes are applied by a growing number of people, and we are healing our planet. It is all based on God and the physics of love. We are learning and applying what works in life.

Since life is a process, a stream of mental moments of awareness containing our life experiences, at any given moment we notice the impact of ignorance in our life and in our world. That point of beginning to notice is enormous.

The impact is huge. As a human race we are concerned about what may happen at this critical juncture. But there is so much hope. The solution is right in front of our eyes. It lies within us. It is to focus our attention solely on love.

We can stop fighting now. We can love the dark as well as the light. We can understand that those who wish to harm us and themselves are acting out of ignorance and fear. Do you have faith in love? Enough faith to love the darkness right out of the world? Believe in your True Self, because it IS happening!

Imagine a big room with a dimmer switch. As you walk in the room it is completely dark. You turn the round knob to the right and slowly the light appears. As you continue to turn the knob, there is more and more light and the objects in the room become clear. When the knob is completely turned to the right, the light is bright and the darkness no longer exists.

The light in our world is awareness. We have much to become aware of as individuals and as a human race. It is our responsibility to share our knowledge with each other. It is our responsibility to realize the path to peace and walk it together.

As we become aware of the dark deeds of ignorance, we can keep a perspective that does not blind us, yet does not let our energy flow to help create more dark deeds. There is freedom in knowing the truth. Truth revealed gives freedom to victims and perpetrators.

We must protect each other. All beings have needs and rights. We must become aware of who is being harmed or wronged. We are here as Warriors of Truth to set free those who need help. We are not bystanders. We are mighty! We can take a stand and use our energy rightly. Right now, although we need to gather our strength and wisdom from within, it is imperative that we take action to stop any harm that is being done that is brought to our awareness.

We can and will resolve the paradox of the need for awareness and the need to focus our attention on solutions and constructive creations.

How We Use Our Attention to Create Our Reality

We are sending energy to whatever we give our attention to. The ideas we entertain in our mind form into physical reality. Our consciousness is light. This light forms the energy in our space into our experiences. Our emotions are energy in motion and it gets formed through our mind into our reality. Strong emotions really empower our thoughts. It's pure physics.

The reason we aren't aware that we are creating our experiences is because there is often so much time between the time we imagine and the time we experience the reality. And there's so much time because we're not focused and conscious in our thinking processes. Up until recently, we have not been aware of how to use our innate creative abilities to their full extent, but we have been using them anyway.

Here's an example of a life experience I created through my thoughts and emotions. I wasn't aware at the time what I was doing, but when I looked back on it, I was amazed. That's why I use this process consciously now.

I was at an amusement park with a friend, my son, and two other children. My friend and I had not been getting along for quite a while and it had become evident to me that separation was imminent. I didn't even want to take this vacation, but since we had promised the kids, we decided to go ahead. While we were in line an incident happened between my son and my friend and we ended up getting into an argument about it and I went one way with my son, and the friend and the other kids went another way.

We went over to a food stand and got something to eat and my son went to get his silhouette painted. I just sat there and cried my eyes out. I had already gone through one heartache right after having adopted a baby. Now I just felt so brokenhearted that a unified family situation wasn't going to work out again. I felt extremely deep emotions. As I was crying, I imagined being picked up as a spirit and taken very far away. I imagined that I was in an exquisite place and that I had a sense of relief. It felt like a wondrous place with lots of beauty where we could heal and have great adventures. I remember a sense of flowers and their sweet aroma all about.

One year later—August 1999—my son and I moved to France near the French Riviera. I had gotten a job with my sister's company as a training specialist at a software development company. In the meantime, the separation occurred and I moved to a new place with my son. I visited France in June and that's when my sister mentioned the new training center they were initiating at the Sophia Antipolis, France office where she worked.

The experience was just like the dream.

The job came with a great salary and many bonuses as well. The company paid tuition at an international school for my son, Jason. We lived in a 5 bedroom villa overlooking the base of the French Alps in a quaint little village. The environment gave me that same feeling I had imagined. When I took walks I used to inhale deeply and feel the release as I exhaled, feeling such a sense of relief. The beauty and essential aromas of flowers were all around in the southern villages of France. I smelled the smoke from burning brush in the fall and the fresh flowers in the spring. We met many wonderful people and saw many great sights in Europe. We certainly had our adventures. It was just like I had imagined, only all the details were filled in.

The essence of the feeling was the same. That's the key.

Once I realized that my imagination had something to do with my future experience, I used the process consciously. Once I decided to create a new place to live. I would periodically sit in the essence of what type of place that I had determined to live in. In perfect timing, the place that had the essence of what I would move into showed up in my experience and I moved into the perfect place.

Attention and Absolute Value

The mathematical concept of absolute value lends some understanding to how our attention affects energy. Whether a number is negative or positive, the absolute value of that number is positive. For example, the absolute value of negative 7 is 7. The absolute value of positive 7 is also 7.

When we give our attention to anti-war energy, energy that is opposing war, we are giving *war* energy. It helps war to exist. Furthermore, we are engaging in a "fight" against war. It is a negative energy.

If we wish for war to stop existing, we can remove our attention from it and place our attention elsewhere. The words of wisdom— "Let It Be"— that the Beatles sang about totally applies here. By just letting things be without giving them our attention neutralizes the energy and allows the unwanted war energy to dissipate.

We can cease actively participating on things that support war, or any other cause we don't support. Some of the great leaders have demonstrated how to peacefully stop supporting wrongful ways by applying civil disobedience. It's the right thing to do.

We create peace by living it.

Targeting our attention toward what we do wish to exist will produce the outcome that we wish to design.

If we wish for peace to exist, then we give peace our attention. That is positive energy. We are shining our light on peace. If we send this energy consciously with strong emotions such as compassion and love, our intent for peace will manifest. It is manifesting now.

Ancient Words of Wisdom: Let It Be

Zero point energy is unconditional love. It is the alpha and the omega, the source and the destination of all creation. Nature springs from this place and returns to it naturally in the cosmic cycle. Our sense of reality shifts and changes through cycles and seasons of time.

In Universal Reality, there is no time. Now exists eternally. We can experience Universal Reality when we get really present in the now moment. We can create our reality from that place when we learn how to channel pure unconditional love. I'll talk more about that later.

Some people don't realize that there is no possible existence without love. They think themselves to be separate from others while entertaining a false sense of personal power. This is Lucifer energy. It's the energy that reels around every so often to try to prove that it can live on its own power—without God or love. There is no sense of Oneness and connection to the whole. Beings who become this energy try to take over. They are greedy, hateful, destructive, deceitful, arrogant, power hungry, and non-caring. They represent the absence or opposite of love. They practice deceit and manipulation to undermine free thinking and free will choice.

This is the most intense ignorance. Although there really is a God spark within these people, they don't realize it because it diminishes without attention. If it weren't there, they wouldn't exist. If they sold their soul for worldly gain, and if they perpetrated crimes against humanity, then maybe someday they won't exist. Since we all have free will, they are allowed to try anything they want. However, Universal Reality is fool-proof!

God is present everywhere and within everyone. There is no place where God is not. God and love are synonymous. With that in mind, imagine someone who is dark-focused. If we sent love to them, that love energy would spark the divinity within that person and their light would grow. They don't have to be aware of it, but they *will* change for the better.

It doesn't make sense to hate the hater. That's feeding dark energy with dark energy. Whoa! Let's stop that in a hurry. We are at a critical juncture on this planet, and if we don't *get* and *apply* concepts such as these quickly, we could be allowing more negativity and destruction and the trampling over of rights and needs while many are harmed or wronged.

There is no reason for fear. We don't ever die. However, we

have a big problem here on earth and we have the means to solve it. That's part of our souls' evolution. Though we are all connected, we determine our own fate by our individual choices.

In any given moment, we have two choices: whether to act out of fear or out of love. Fear can be broken down to mean any negative emotion. Some of them are: jealousy, anger, arrogance, superiority, or hate. Love can be seen in many forms as well: compassion, concern, acceptance, understanding, forgiveness, grace, mercy, and kindness to name a few.

If our attention is focused on the light of love, then we grow spiritually. Our Source is within. We express it in our thoughts, words, and actions. If our attention is focused on the dark side, or our old programming based in fear, then we spiral downwards in consciousness and our inner light wanes until we wake up.

We all have a combination of dark and light. When we shift to an awareness and lifestyle of conscious evolution and live from our heart, we pay attention to our light. We know what is light by what feels good to our deeper self. We know if we are being true to our Self. During our transformation we are more conscious of our old way of being that no longer serves our True Selves' highest good, and what does not. We are in the midst of change. We accept ourselves where we are at, and allow the space to grow into our True Divinity.

Paying Attention to our Soul

There are varying levels of awareness of our spiritual nature, but most people do realize that our soul lives on after we die, so I'm going to start there. How much have you contemplated or researched what happens to our souls after we die? Sometimes the perspective is that we can't know what happens to our soul after we die until we actually do, so the contemplation just stops there.

However, we are designed to discern the truth about any matter for which we feel compelled to know. When we read or hear something that is true, we can get a strong "gut feeling" that it is true or false.

Sometimes we even get "truth chills" when we feel the cells of our bodies tingle. We have a deep inner knowingness of the truth that we can access consciously.

This is not the same as when the information meets our belief system and our thought processes around that ensue. The difference is that Universal Truth is constant and our belief systems are subjective and subject to change.

Reconcile: Casting Light Upon the Shadows for Healing and Focusing on Intentional Creations

While it is true that we are powerful creators and focusing on what we do want to exist is optimal, we do have shadows to heal. We need the light of our awareness and hence a bit of our attention to make this healing happen.

What is the gist of our emotional energy behind the attention we are "paying" as energy? This is where our skills of transmutation are important to recognize, and apply.

We are becoming aware of such atrocities of child sex trafficking, pedophilia, and satanic ritual abuse. Oh, how it hurts our hearts! It seems so difficult to bear such a burden on the soul to accept that such things have been happening. And yet, it would be wrong to let it continue. We have to place our attention on these issues to solve them.

This is a big job for humanity!

This we must change at once.

It is part the process of evolving to manage such a great challenge. We definitely need to pray, to find the ones who are being abused and free them from this situation and from the people who do this, and to offer healing. We need to identify and stop the perpetrators. They need to be restrained and reformed. The perpetrators can confess what led them down the wrong road, and then right themselves by doing good in the world. But will they all repent? That's up to them and God. Our job is to protect our children, and we can do it with all the mama bear might in our hearts. And we will.

The answer is Unconditional love for all. It's hard to apply sometimes, but it *is* the answer.

We can lift our vision for each soul. We can imagine they are achieving their highest potential. We can see each one living from the highest truth and the purest love. We can see each one contributing to the world with their unique gifts and talents. We can see them having meaning and purpose in their lives that gives them vitality and enthusiasm. We can see our world where goodwill toward all prevails.

We have all missed the mark at times; we have all failed to be our best and we have made mistakes. We can help someone who has fallen down to get back up instead of judging them. We can be like an older brother or sister and set a good example. Rather than accuse, we can help.

We do not ignore it, nor do we allow harm to come to others. We take a stand. We come in strength. We have the courage to speak the truth in spite of the potential consequences. We do it with full knowing we could give our lives to our Divine cause of protecting our children.

Those who do such dark deeds are murderers, plain and simple. But although they may take our lives, they have *no power* to take our souls.

We are powerful souls.

So the answer to the paradox is: give all your energy to righteousness, or right use of energy. Intentions to help, uplift, and liberate others from harm is not the same as giving energy to what we don't wish to create. It is using the light of awareness to heal the shadows of humanity.

It takes a big heart and a lot of courage to tackle the problems of today. We can use the love in our hearts to resurrect the shadows into the full potential of Divinity by transmuting the energy and situation, transcending the dark sight of evil and replacing it with a higher vision that represents a positive potential, and transform darkness to light.

We are traversing the shift between the old paradigm and the new paradigm. The truth will subjugate and dissolve the old paradigm. Being strong and courageous and taking righteous action when needed is essential. But at the same time that we are taking down the old empires of the outdated power structures, we are building a new world of a peaceful heaven on earth with our new expanded and empowered consciousness.

As we straddle these two paradigms of reality, we may be researching and spreading truth at some times, and creating something new to replace the old systems at other times. Both of these aspects are part of our mission. We are definitely multitasking!

Attention, Distraction, and True Freedom

We are endowed by our Creator with freedom of mind. Our mind creates our reality. As a whole, humanity has lost its ability to see the connection with aspects of consciousness, primarily thoughts and feelings, and the experiences and circumstances in our lives. Through Divine Grace and intervention, we are now re-awakening to our true creative powers.

This is an opportunity to reassess our lives and our world and to change whatever it is that does not resonate with our true being. We can put an end to suffering. We can put an end to poverty and debt. We can put an end to illusions and experiences of lack. We can put an end to corruption and medical tyranny.

We can experience optimum health. We can replace and transform the old institutions with new models that are instilled with honest transparency, good morals, sturdy values, high ethical standards, and beneficial impacts on all persons involved or affected. This change IS happening.

Humanity as a whole and each of us individually is experiencing cognitive dissonance, or stress, when we are not in alignment with our true power of mind.

By becoming aware of our inherent freedom of mind, how to reclaim it, and how to harness its creative powers, we can be set free to create and experience our lives and our world according to our true hearts' desires. First, we have to realize and end the usurpation of our attention. We have to understand the ways that deceit has been used to act against our better judgment. We have to recognize and reject relative moralism and all of the schemes to change our inherent God-based values. We need to really wake up to the fight of evil against the bodies, minds, and souls of humanity.

When we regain control of our own minds, we can experience abundance and fulfillment. We can tap into the power of our soul, know truth, and consciously direct our minds. We can discover our individual gifts and put meaning and purpose into our lives using the creative freedom that is our birthright. This is Universal Order and it will bring peace and harmony to our planet.

Through societal conditioning, our values and awareness has become skewed. Our minds have been like ping pong balls, bouncing here and there, directed and re-directed through outer forces. We have not retained the awareness of the power of our minds and hearts. We have relinquished our individual sovereignty. We have become distracted from purposeful living. We have developed the belief that life is happening to us rather than through us. We have devolved to victim consciousness.

It doesn't cost anything to take our mind back.

Time to Reclaim Freedom of Mind

The first principle to understand when reclaiming freedom of mind is the conscious direction of attention. Normally, we direct our attention outwardly most of the time. Unless we meditate or contemplate regularly, our awareness is observing outer reality. We need to spend regular periods of time directing our attention inwardly to access the power of our soul-our true self. By tapping into our inner wisdom we apprehend truth. We become empowered by our essential nature of spirit. We receive guidance and direction for our lives and we discover our individual gifts and reason for being.

When we are attuned to our innermost being, we know truth because we are one with it. Then we get the cognitive dissonance that sends us down rabbit holes of research. In this process our discernment is developed. We are critical thinkers when we claim independent minds and engage in independent thinking. WE control our minds and our attention. WE determine what is or is not true, and what WE wish to create. We make our own visions.

What we place our attention on is where our energy goes. It also programs our memory. If we become conscious of what we are doing with our attention and the impact it has on our life, we can become inspired to make some beneficial changes.

Societal conditioning has occurred by design. If we can be deceived to give up our freedom of mind, then others can control us. They can usurp our personal power, and they can greedily accumulate the world's wealth of resources through selfish motives and deceptive strategies. It's been happening for a very long time. Technologies are being used in harmful ways that destroy, rather than support, life on our planet. There is much to be brought into our awareness here so that we can rise above it. We can learn to succeed with true values and by using our greater inner technologies.

There has been purposeful programming of our subconscious minds through commercials that contain subliminal messages and symbols. There has been values programming by making us believe our being and our value is determined by what we have. Our perceptions have been manipulated to serve the few rather than the greater good of the whole. Waking up to the truth about these issues is helping to impress the importance of the changes we need to make to become empowered by freedom of mind once again.

Geoengineering, H.A.A.R.P., the pharmaceutical drug push, media manipulation through narratives, weather warfare, biowarfare, radiation, and EMF waves from cell phone technologies that are meant to harm or destroy us have no power over us if we master our own minds and vibration. The frequencies of love are scientifically proven to provide better health and welfare. Attune to the frequencies of Earth by going out into nature. Understand the Schumann resonance factor for your health and well-being. Your mind will respond. Your body will become healthy.

Distraction

Distraction is a method of capturing attention and energy. Have you ever had a goal or something you wanted to accomplish and then got distracted? What did you do to eliminate distractions to accomplish your goal? Have you ever "set your mind" to get something done, and then did it?

Imagine eliminating all distractions and focusing your attention on your intended outcomes. Practice setting some intentions and then focus your attention on achieving it, use your mind (attention), your heart (feelings of passion), and your body (physical action) to accomplish your goal. Inside you will feel the intrinsic value (joy, happiness, peace) of being in alignment with your True Self.

Awareness is not a matter of ignoring the truth. It simply places the negative effects of what has been created into the periphery vision of the mind, moving into the causal nature of the mind and whole consciousness, to create something better. Awareness is powerful. We just can't dwell on what's wrong all the time. We need to put into our minds what we are going to replace it with. We are becoming conscious creators.

Tricks and Traps

Watch out for the tricks and traps that cause delusion for your soul. Once you realize your True God Self through Oneness, or Unity with God, through communion and matching and maintaining the pure vibration of love with integrity of conscience, you will not be likely to fall into these traps. But if these are mentioned here, you may be alert to the warnings and signs of such traps.

Faith or Inferiority Complex

When you believe in your True God Self, that divine spark within that you pay attention to with your heart and mind and soul and strength, you develop perfect faith. But on the path of development, we get feedback or programming that is detrimental to our self-worth, or self-esteem. Before we are fully developed, we sometimes buy into these thoughts and embed them in our subconscious minds.

Be alert and aware that these types of input are not of God. They are not the truth. We don't need to buy into labels, or put downs of any kind. Stay away from naysayers. Don't speak to them about your dreams and aspirations. Ignore any verbiage that makes you feel like anything less than a perfect Child of God. Stand up for yourself! You can simply say in your mind or out loud: "That is not my truth."

Self-talk is very important. Speak highly of yourself. Even when you make mistakes, don't call yourself names or belittle yourself out loud or in your mind. Acknowledge you did not do the best thing, or make the best decision, and vow to do better. Accept it as a valuable lesson. Be grateful for what you learned. We all make mistakes. It's part of our learning process. Forgive yourself, and you can forgive others. Love yourself unconditionally, and then you can love others unconditionally. It all starts at home, inside the heart and mind. We are conscious beings as we monitor and upgrade our thoughts and feelings, consistently striving to keep our thoughts positive and our feelings pure. "I am the resurrection and the life." That is a great transmutational tool to uplift the vibrations of the heart and mind. Another one is gratitude. "I am grateful to be a Child of God; I am one with God's pure love and infinite knowing of Truth."

Ask for perfect faith. We can always ask for help. That's the beauty of Oneness Awareness. "All for one and one for all." We are unified in consciousness, all tuned in to the God vibration, and we communicate through a two way channel. We are heard and answered. Our calls for answers or solutions can't possibly go unnoticed. My favorite lesson is that "God is imminent and responsive." I've read the literature of Paramahansa Yogananda extensively and have received great benefits to my soul. He is partners, as such, with Jesus. I asked Jesus for perfect faith that he demonstrates in his life expression. I can't say where I would be today if it weren't for asking for help. I am truly grateful. We are each blessed in that way.

Egotism/vanity or Glory to God

Before you toot your own horn, or puff yourself up, think again. Where did you receive your life energy? Where did you receive your ideas? From where did you receive your inspiration? From where did you receive your strength? It all comes from God. Give God the glory, the credit for all good that you are, and all good that you do. That is the Truth.

The world likes to trap those that are egotistical or narcissistic through their pride and vanity. They are easy targets. They are the low hanging fruit for the evil ones. With fancy titles and positions of power and large financial payoffs, these vain and narcissistic souls with pride and avarice are easy targets to turn into the minions of the evil ones. These lost souls do the bidding of the dark forces. They think very highly of themselves. They tend to disregard the laws of God. They harm people and take away their freedoms. Woe unto them.

During this time of soul ripening, we get tested. Our tests consist of either falling into these tricks and traps or doing the right thing. Look at the people in hospitals who are doing the bidding of the dark evil ones by following tyrannical medical protocols that kill many of the patients, but yield the corporate overlords huge sums of money. Look at all the doctors and nurses who have exposed the truth, quit their jobs, and/or started freedom organizations and movements to educate and free the people from this tyranny by exposing the truth.

When you are tuned to the God vibration, the perfect choice is obvious. It is repulsive to your soul to go along with harmful activities. Without vanity or egotism, we come from love—we love our children, we love each other, we love life. I see the world waking up. I'm watching, as well as participating, in the great stand for truth. People are answering the call of their soul that is fired up with the passion of righteousness. Instead of falling for the tyranny, the global population is taking a stand.

There are still some at the time of this writing that are going along in ignorance. They have misplaced trust. They trust all doctors, the media, the government, all churches and pastors, and the corporations. Their numbers are dwindling. I hope by the time you read this, that a major shift has taken place. If so, celebrate! That time will come.

Secrets, lies, or partial truth vs. Whole Truth: The Knowledge of God

Knowing God is knowing truth. It is the key to our personal realization of our True Self, and the key to our sovereignty. Our perfect faith comes from KNOWING. When you know, you know. It doesn't matter what anybody else says. When you have that direct contact with spirit and that deep peace and love that is undeniable within then you have that rock of unity with God.

There is strength of character that comes from knowing God. There is a natural humility and honesty that result from knowing our Father. United with God, the soul knows discernment. If we are ever unsure, we just ask. The answer always comes.

If anyone tries to deceive, or coerce, or lie, or keep secrets, our connection with God lets us know within. We seek answers, and we find answers. When we are delivered a partial truth, our inner knowing gets nudged and we feel funny. Our spidey senses of intuitive knowing makes us search for the whole truth.

When we don't know if something is true or not we can find out in due time. The whole human population is attuning to truth and that's why there is so much exposure happening. Jesus said that truth will subjugate the world. Well, that is happening now. Suppression of truth cannot last. The great global revival is the masses turning to God because we demand the whole truth, and nothing but the truth. Because of the vast increase in our spiritual evolution, we don't buy into the propaganda or sugar-coated schemes of deception. Only the whole truth will set us free.

We won't stand for anything less. Praise God!

True Freedom

We can experience true freedom by continually attuning to our inner core—to our soul self through our heart with inward attention. This attunement is a calibration of consciousness. It connects us to the genius intelligence within. It is time for humanity to collectively regain control of our freedom of mind. Suffering cannot continue. Oppressive forces cannot remain hidden and attempt to control our minds for us.

Individually we must make the choice and the effort to regain control of our mind. We can do this through conscious attention direction, elimination of distractions, and focusing our attention on solutions provided through the intelligence of the soul.

Let us master our minds and be free!

Become a Master of Personal Life Energy

The best way to change the world is to change ourselves. Large numbers of people are modifying their way of being tremendously. The world IS changing big time as a result.

We go straight to source and get unlimited energy. We go for wisdom and guidance. We attune to God's will to live in harmony with the universe and to perceive our soul's blueprint and fulfill our personal mission for our part in the Divine Plan. We relate to higher realms and cooperate with higher beings to unfold our own potential and assist in creating God's perfect image of Heaven into physical form. We perceive our mission, our life's purpose, and know where we are needed at any given time. We receive unlimited supplies of abundance.

We communicate information through images, our imagination combined with our willful intentions and the feeling generated from our heart. We go deep, we practice, and our faith in the process increases as we experience reliable results.

By strengthening our faith, we become masters.

A strong Divine connection is more precious than gold. In fact, it provides the alchemy to transform lower vibrations to higher vibrations, bring light to darkness, and to make the world a better place.

Unity and Cooperation

With our Divine connection secure and in place, we organically unite with others of the same high vibration of love. Since we are one with Father God, our Source of infinite intelligence and love, it is natural to engage in loving cooperation with others to make the world a better place.

Just by setting clear intentions and then following our inner guidance and the signs of synchronicity, we flow into patterns of unity. We are organized naturally to perform our life missions with those who are like-hearted and like-minded and are navigated with clear direction by pathways formed power of will in our spirit born intentions.

Families are born all the time! They grow, they change, and they last for the season of the completion of the divine intentions. New cycles begin following the ending or completion of a spiritual purpose. There is never need for goodbyes because we are all unified in one spirit and we cycle back to each other in due season. Love never dies.

With joy and celebration we are creating and enjoying the vision and unfoldment of Heaven on Earth together. We are bonded tightly in the vibration of love. It just keeps getting better!

Chapter Seven

CYCLES OF LOVE

Love applied in every moment is our highest destiny.

What is Love?

How can you define love? Have you ever tried? It's one of those questions that you instinctively know the answer to, but putting it into words or giving it a definition seems to minimize it in some way. It seems like defining it would put to it in a container that could never be large enough. Love is so big it reaches out to infinity. Just the geography of it is astronomical!

If we tried to describe the geography of everything that is enveloped by love, we would have a huge job on our hands. If we sent out agents to describe every place in the universe (or try infinity!), it would take zillions of people. Each person would come back and explain their portion of exploration the way they saw and experienced it in that location. The answer would be different based on the nature of their location and their experience of it. All answers would be different, and yet they would all be right about their own experience. And so it is with love. We each experience it differently.

Love holds everything within it and creates perfect order. Love attracts.

Love is a binding force that holds the universe together. It holds people together, too, and that's how we experience it the most. When we sense love between ourselves and another person, we feel close to that person. We feel a bond. Feeling love within feels warm and connecting. Expressing love strengthens its binding force and inherently makes us feel good inside.

Conversely, love is also freedom. Love is so free that its nature would not even let us put it into the box of a definition. When we truly love someone, we give them the total freedom to be who they are. That's how God loves us. We have inherent free will. Is there any withholding of love on the part of God, no matter how we use our free will? Absolutely not! Even if we commit the most heinous crime, we are treated with compassion and are guided by the balance of feeling what it's like to be on the other side of those actions by the welcomed lessons of karma. We experience unconditional love in the whole process of our soul's evolution. That is Divine Love.

When we love someone, we don't always feel a warm fuzzy feeling. We are committed to loving that person no matter what, and then we step outside our own comfort zone to be what another needs us to be so that they can experience our love throughout their own growth period. This is a God-like aspect of ourselves that we develop as we evolve. We are expressing unconditional love.

Expressions of love can come in an infinite variety. A smile. A kind word. A gentle touch. Hugs. Kisses. Holding a hand. Intimacy. Caring by showing up and being present with somebody. Sharing what we are or what we have. The creation of fun experiences. Humor. An infinitude of kind acts. Tolerance. Understanding. These are just a few general concepts of love expressions. Specific expressions of love are held in moments and stories of eons, held in the hearts of our souls.

In fact, it is the evolutionary process of our soul to realize that love is our nature and love is our goal. It really holds the answer to everything. Self-realization can be described as the true knowingness, expression, and experience of the love that we are. As we become self realized, ultimately we dissolve duality into the beingness of pure love and meld into Source. In the meantime, we enjoy the process because the illusion of separation and duality gives us a broader base to experience love. It's the whole reason for life.

It doesn't matter what we do in life—our success is ultimately determined by how much we love. The fruit of our life is the expression of our love. If our ideal of ourselves would be to express pure unconditional love in every moment, we could really clean up our act and live life more fully. We would experience a rich and fulfilling life. We are on the path of the perfect fruition of love right now.

The Natural Cycle of Love

We are here to develop and express the love that we are. We grow in our capacity to give and receive love from the inception of our souls.

God is love. We are children of God. We *are* love. Realizing that we are love helps us to find true lasting happiness. From the premise of that realization, we can start to love God, ourselves, and others. Feeling love brings us joy. Expressing love brings us joy.

The cycle of love begins with God, our Source. When we realize God loves us unconditionally and lean on the divine love of Spirit, we learn how we also can love in that way. It takes much time and practice because when we experience relationships that aren't generating love toward us, we are programmed in a way to react—an eye for an eye kind of philosophy. However, if we love back instead, we break that cycle. Love is bigger than anything. It can heal any relationship. Sometimes it has to be done from a distance, but it still works.

Understanding helps. If we understand that each person is acting according to their best idea of how life works, and that there is always a reason for them being the way they are, or doing whatever they do, then we can forgive them without having to know exactly why they did something to understand them. When a baby messes their diapers, people automatically understand that they just don't know any better yet. We are all at different stages of development, and if someone acts with less than kind regard, we too can demonstrate the understanding that they just don't know any better yet. Let's love them anyway.

I remember practicing that general type of understanding when I was in traffic. If someone was going super slow and it annoyed me, I would say to myself: "if that were someone I knew, I would just understand them and why they were like that, so instead of getting mad, I'm just going to love them." Also, when someone made a mistake and pulled out in front of me because they weren't being very aware, I would think to myself "I remember times when I had something heavily on my mind and did something stupid, too. I'll just forgive them and love them anyway." I'd like to add, this was not my original reaction! I used to get mad and swear a lot when I was in traffic. But as I began to consciously evolve and my resolve was to love everybody, I found that driving in traffic was one of my biggest challenges and one of my biggest opportunities for growth in loving people I didn't know.

It's easier to love someone you know, because you really understand them. Typically we know our family members and close friends the best. That's where most people place and practice their love.

As we evolve, so does our capacity to love. We learn what experiences feel like—from both sides of each type of action eventually—so we learn and become determined not to feel or cause pain.

At the beginning of the process, the cycle of love, we learn to love our parents and siblings and close friends. Our sense of self grows and we feel bonded. In school we have our sports teams, clubs, or project teams and we feel bonded and a sense of belonging at *our* school. So we love the people we go to school with and continue by relating with others among our community and groups or other organizations we belong to. Our sense of self and our capacity to love grows even further as our relationships evolve.

As we grow older, we become more responsible and take part in governing our country by voting and participating in the activities of our culture. We become attuned to the group and sense our belonging to our country. Our sense of self grows to a national level. Although we don't agree with everyone in our group or country, we continue to relate and evolve through our relationships; defining who we are and what we stand for, while continuing to expand our capacity to love. When our country is at war or gets attacked, we feel a bond born of compassion for everyone in our nation, setting aside personal opinions and differences. Our capacity to love grows even further. In our current precipice, we are battling the darkness with light even within our homes and nations, but that just causes us to sharpen the instrument of love. We are united by our swords of truth that now stretch globally.

Eventually, we realize we are part of the whole organism of earth of which humanity is a part. We have a larger sense of self associated with the belonging and participation of life on planet Earth. We hone our relationships and begin to care ever deeper for our environment and our fellow man. Eventually we deeply realize and sense our Oneness. Our sense of self is expanded and we love all.

That is our outer expression of our growing capacity to experience and express love.

Our inner experience includes the growing love for ourselves. Once we truly learn to unconditionally love others, we find we are really harder on ourselves than anybody. It is then we call on God. Do we feel separate or do we feel God's unconditional love? That is our choice and our lesson. Once we do feel God's unconditional love for us, we learn to forgive ourselves until finally we realize, there's nothing to forgive. We are in a perfect process of life. We can grow up at our own pace and we will always be loved—always, no matter what—by God, our Source.

So the whole evolution of love begins and ends with God. God raises us individually and loves us unconditionally. Whether we realize it or not, there's nothing but God in-between as well--coaching us, guiding us, directing us, loving us. Love is really all there is, contracting and expanding with the breath of the universe.

Comprehensive Unconditional Love

If we could all love every person, place, and thing in every moment sincerely in our hearts and if all of our thoughts, words, and actions came from that intentional love, then life on our planet would be better instantly. We would raise the quality of our experience individually as we benefit every life we touch with our expressions of kindness and compassion. The joy that we would experience would come deep from within our souls and we would know why we came to live this life in the first place.

Love can't be defined or seen with the naked eye, and yet, it's the Source of all that is *really* real.

Acceptance: The Key That Opens the Door

As we set out to create a life and a world that is based in love rather than fear, on understanding rather than control, on cooperation rather than competition, on sharing rather than hoarding, on healing rather than harming, on creating rather than destroying, on harmony rather than conflict, and ultimately on peace rather than war, it will lead to experiences in all of our lives where we feel peace and harmony. Everyone will have the realization that there is plenty for everyone and the planet will be healed from pollution and depletion and we will live and let live in the spirit of love. We have to start where we are first.

As an individual, when you are experiencing anything other than love, you can simply make a perception adjustment and get back to the source of your true nature and your innermost desire: unconditional love itself. It may seem easier said than done, but with proven step-by-step instructions, you can make this process your own and experience it for yourself. When you try it and get used to it with practice, then you, too, will say it is simple.

First, the acceptance principles will be explained, and then an example of a real life application will be relayed. There will be exercises that follow for specific applications of using the key of acceptance. Exercise 1 is about realizing God's acceptance, understanding, and unconditional love for you. Exercise 2 is about how to accept, understand, and love yourself as is during the process of development. Exercise 3 instructs you how to accept, understand, and love someone else. Exercise 4 is about how to accept, understand, and love our whole life and all of our present circumstances. Exercise 5 is about how to accept, understand, and love our world as it is. (See *Bulls-Eye Faith Inner Work Book* for more details.)

The first thing to accept is that you are part of a whole. Although you don't control anyone or anything besides yourself, you do control yourself with the choices you make and by directing your attention. The choices you make do have a substantial impact on who and what's around you, but you are not in control of directing the whole. In the first exercise you will realize at a deeper level that you are part of a whole, and come to accept the individuated, interrelated part that you are.

Anything that you experience as something you don't like can be thought of as negative, or as resistance. It's an energy that you resist in the form of your self, or a person, or a circumstance in your life. Resistance can feel like anger, annoyance, disgust, repulsiveness, jealousy, anxiety, stress, superiority, inferiority, pity, or any other negative thought or emotion. It is being out of harmony with our self, another person (or people), or a circumstance in your life such as where you work or live or your health or finances.

On the other side of the line is love; it can be thought of as positive. Mentally, love is experienced as wisdom. Emotionally, love is felt as a warm bonding feeling of unity; a deep sense of belonging to the whole. Physically, love is experienced as peaceful, joyous, or exuberant energy. Spiritually, love is sensed as joyful bliss. It is a completely satiated soul. Environmentally and universally, love is felt as peace and harmony.

In order to pass from negative to positive, we go right through zero point, which is neutral. We do this with acceptance.

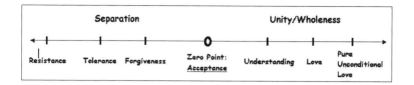

When there is a negative charge, you sense separation from the whole. The more you feel love, the more you feel the bond of unity and wholeness.

Acceptance is just noticing the facts objectively without any charge. You can lose the charge by changing your perception, or your point of awareness. As soon as you notice that you are not feeling peace and harmony, you can consciously shift your perception of the moment.

You do this by consciously putting yourself in an observer role. As you step back, your awareness becomes broader. You just look at "what is" objectively. The energy neutralizes. You can observe yourself, or you can step back even farther and become the observer of your observer. The farther you step back, the more objective you can be and the more perspectives you can check out to create a broader understanding. The more understanding you acquire, the more love you feel.

When we feel resistance, we are really sensing a core fear. What everyone fears the most is not being loved. We fear not being understood. We fear not being accepted as we are. Since the core essence of your being is love, and that is the binding force of the universe in which you are an integral part, it is that love that you desire. This is what satisfies your soul. Love then, is your ultimate goal.

You can find love within yourself and become totally fulfilled without having to search for it in the outer circumstances of your life, like from other people, for example. You will change from seeking love on the outside to acquire happiness, to accessing the love from your core being which fulfills you and makes you happy, and then you will generously give love since it is so abundantly present within you.

When you stop totally resisting and spewing negative energy such as anger or judgment and become tolerant, you still feel a major separation. There is an inherent lack of understanding that shows that we don't honor those we can only tolerate. Tolerance is usually reserved for people or whole groups of people who have cultures or values that we don't understand or share. People who are tolerant still feel threatened by this other group—they somehow think that their values could undermine their own happiness. There is some judgment in tolerance, but it gets put aside to live civilly and peacefully. Tolerance reflects some residual resistance in our consciousness, or our minds. Our heart is not yet totally open.

Your resistance softens as you choose to forgive those who you feel have damaged or harmed you. You may realize that you love them anyway, or you may come to understand their side of the story. This you do for specific cases, or people you know well. However, if we adopt the general understanding that each person is making choices for their own happiness according to their understanding of how life works, we eventually realize there is nothing to forgive. If someone is acting unconsciously, without consideration of the impact on others, then they just don't know any better. Jesus understood that when he spoke of his persecutors saying: "Forgive them, for they know not what they do." It is this realization that helps you to move forward into acceptance a lot faster.

These are the times on our planet that we are all clearing all old fears, negative thought patterns, and old outdated beliefs. Some of these energies have created physical matter in the form of dis-ease in our bodies; some have formed into dis-ease on our planet. We can take each of these energetic entities—accept, love, and understand them, and come out on the other side of that process as pure creative loving beings on a peaceful, harmonious planet where we experience love, beauty, and joy in our every moment. It may sound like a dream, but once we all understand the basis of our God-given creative powers, it is exactly what can come to pass.

Resisting resistance is resistance all the same. You can even accept and understand your "stuff" that comes up that creates resistance.

You can love it for the purpose it has served in the past, and then release it with the realization that you no longer need it. Again, begin by just noticing it and accepting that it exists.

Be willing to accept, understand and love the past and then let go of it and what it has held. Be open to change, open to possibilities, open to new ideas. With an open mind and an open heart, you will truly create your life with the highest degree of quality and enjoyment. Acceptance is the beginning.

When you come across something that bothers you, something that you don't like, you can process it and change how you think and feel inside to create a change in your outer life. In order to move through the wall of pain, sorrow, or negative thoughts or feelings, we need first to utilize the acceptance key that opens the door.

A process is presented here that is very helpful in moving through the consciousness shift that is occurring naturally as we evolve in these transitional times. This process involves feeling accepted by God, accepting ourselves, accepting others or our life circumstances, accepting our whole life as God, and then accepting the world as it is. Accepting in each of these areas begins the transformation of negative or resistance energy in terms of thoughts and feelings into understanding and love.

Using this tool of acceptance, we move through the resistance energies and come back to a feeling of inner peace and love. We feel this for ourselves, for others, and for God. Acceptance is an element of alchemy that creates positive change.

We can create with it in the moment. Love is both the means to the end and the end itself. Being still—being completely present in the now moment—and sensing the love that is always present, the love that *we are* in essence, puts us in the role of creator. Acceptance gains us peace in the now moment when negative or resistance energy threatens our consistent experience of love. It truly is the key that opens the door.

Acceptance helps to create the stillness to be aware of our oneness with God. God is love. God is source energy. God is presence. Being present with unconditional love brings out the God in us.

The transformation of negative energy through acceptance and into love makes us feel less contracted and more expanded. We feel less stress and more peace. We feel totally at ease with our self and with our life. We have more love to apply to any person or circumstance in our life.

You are here to experience love. You can be in the flow of love either by giving it *or* receiving it. The more you give, the more you receive. You have it to give from within you, and as energy moves through you from within or from without, you can transform it back into love with this process that begins with acceptance.

In order to be and express love, we must first really learn to love ourselves.

How To Love Your Self

Initially we think of ourselves as this unique life expression that is built around the story of our life. This is what we call the little, or egoic self. We identify ourselves by what is outside of us. For example, I was born as a white female American in the Midwest whose parents claimed to be Protestant. I say claimed to be because we hardly ever went to church, but at the time a common question was "What religion are you?" and it seemed an answer was necessary. My father committed suicide when I was 5 and my mother went to work to support her four kids. Then my mom married my step-dad who had 2 kids of his own. They had one more together, so we had a family of 9. I went to school, played with my friends and grew up having all sorts of experiences. These initial facts along with all of my experiences became my life story—an identity of who I was. We all have our stories and the associated baggage of feelings and psychic stuff that we carry as long as we identify with them.

As we evolve, we realize our true nature as spirit. But what does that mean, really? What does it feel like to be natural in the moment and sense our true nature? It's a process of discovery. It requires moments of still, quiet time. It calls for being present and feeling

Presence. Creating that time for ourselves changes everything. We realize the nature of our pure essence along with all of the virtues of our soul, and we change. We begin to reflect these virtues in our outer expressions. We realize that wisdom and love are the basis of our true nature – that we truly are God-like beings made in His image. We realize that we are infinite wisdom, pure unconditional love, and powerfully creative. With that realization, we begin to love ourselves.

The more we spend in quiet still time, the more we express our true nature in our outer lives. Our sense of self expands as we realize that our consciousness is part of this huge expansive whole, and we begin to love others as ourselves as a matter of factual sensation, not because someone has told us that we are all one, but because we really know and experience it inside. We become more and more kind and forgiving to ourselves and to others. We experience a more peaceful, loving life as we go about the business of discovering our life purpose and gaining motivation and momentum to do what we came here to do as individuals; connecting with the souls we came here to work with and accomplishing our life's mission. We discover a deep, lasting happiness that is not dependent on outer circumstances, but at the same time being more in control of what they are because of realizing and exercising our creative powers. My mission is to teach this transformative process and to realize and share how to use our creative powers. Life energy, once understood, can be used to help us become and create whatever we desire as we evolve in the process.

Creating a life inclusive of personal quiet time allows us to know ourselves and love ourselves at the very deepest level. A healing process takes place where we say goodbye to all of our old programs, patterns, and beliefs that revolved around our life stories. As we are healed, we have a new outlook on life including an understanding of our Self that allows us to experience unconditional love. Our sense of Self expands and eventually our little egoic self melts away and we *know* everything we think, say, and do affects the whole larger Self of which we are a part. Not only do we love ourselves more, but we love others more with our new deep sense of oneness.

Our depth of sensing our true nature is ever increasing. With conscious intentions realized through sensing our soul in our quiet time we become rich—rich with love, peace, wisdom, clarity, kindness, compassion, creativity, goodwill, generosity, and harmony--expansive in every way. We express these virtues of our soul as we create our unique expression of our true nature. When we express the virtues of our soul we get verification from spirit that we are in resonance with our innermost pure goodness with the sense of intrinsic value. It's a deep feeling of knowing that we are in tune with our soul, or our highest good. We love ourselves more and more using this process. It becomes the path to true lasting happiness that we are all seeking, but often not realizing how to direct our attention to make it so. As we direct our attention inside and express the light of our beingness outside, we experience a deep love of our expanded sense of Self. We experience the love that we seek; the love that we are.

Now that we are moving forward with a foundation of love, it is helpful to dissipate any old negative energies from the past. For this we apply the aspect of love called forgiveness.

Healing With Forgiveness

Imagine feeling like you are completely free and peaceful inside with the most fertile environment for love and joy to exist. Imagine being free of health issues, money worries, relationship concerns, and any form of guilt or self-trashing. Take a moment and really take a deep breath and relax and imagine this complete feeling of freedom. Feel gratitude for this feeling of freedom. Just be with it for a few minutes.

Doesn't it feel great? If you would like to expand that feeling from a tiny moment into a permanent way of existence, absorb this message about forgiveness and see what kind of relief you feel in your life.

Although at first this may sound impossible when you consider the reality of your life, if you think about it, the one thing that you do control is you—how you think and feel inside. Your inner world creates your outer reality.

As we live our lives we experience drama that causes us to learn and grow through the challenges of life. That's what life is for. However, we don't have to be so imbedded in the drama that we forget to use our inherent power to change things for the better or to realize we created this drama for the purpose of our own evolution. A higher perspective often contains the key to relief.

Right now I have a son and I am a single mother. I got married when I was 24, hoping to have children as soon as possible. I really loved my husband a lot and dreamed of spending my whole life with him. We got along great and shared many interests and friends. Getting pregnant wasn't as easy as I had anticipated and fertility was a major issue. I had a tubal pregnancy and a few miscarriages along with much medical probing and surgical procedures, but to no avail. Years kept creeping by as my friends had baby after baby. I felt deep emotional pain. This poem I wrote back then describes the feelings I was having:

Where's My Baby

Years have sailed right past me
As I express the same old cry
I want to have a baby
Real soon, before I die

There's a place deep within my heart
That yearns to be fulfilled
Its emptiness cries out to me
Only a baby's love will yield

I see the other mothers
How happy they seem to be
I hold their infant so close with love
But their bond is not with me

The daddies are so proud
As their eyes gleam with joy
I sure would like to see my husband
With our little girl or little boy

But time keeps going by me
I'm disappointed every month
I want to have a baby
I really need to so much

The scenes in life remind me
When I see parents and children play
I know exactly what I'm missing
I want my life that way

But years keep going by me
As my friends have their second or third
I keep asking "Where's my baby?"
But my pain is never cured

God, I know you care for me
I live to do Your will
But I pray to have a baby (soon)
For my heart is crying still

Finally, after 8 years of marriage, we adopted our son. I was ecstatic! Finally we had a family. Unfortunately it didn't last long. We had received our son in March and in December divorce suddenly became imminent. I was devastated.

Since then, I faced many difficult challenges. These challenges just drove me to rely on God more and my inner resources. I prayed a lot and read a lot of spiritual uplifting literature. During the transition of becoming a single parent, I finished my bachelor's degree in Elementary Education with a 3.97 grade point average and graduated with honors. I started my teaching career in elementary school, and ended up teaching middle school for many years. I began raising my son alone when he was five years old. My son and I lived through it all and we overcame all the tough times and had lots of good times, too. We are very close to this day.

My experiences lead me to lessons of forgiveness.

I found a poem recently about unconditional love that I had written about my depth of love. It goes like this:

I Love You

I love you unconditionally
No matter what you do
I love you just the way you are
Just for being you

I love you when you're happy
And even when you're sad
I love you at your very best
And when you think you're bad

And love is what you give me
Through everything we share
Our lives are rich with one another
And one another cares

Since I've been in a place of conscious personal transformation, especially the last few years, I've been open to changing myself and becoming bigger than my life circumstances. When incidents occurred that caused emotional pain and it brought my attention to the need to forgive, I processed the pain within. I paid attention to synchronistic events as they always point to a direction that improves my life.

Once I was at a friend's house and she asked me to pick an angel card. The card was "Forgiveness" saying that the angels were asking me to forgive someone. At first I didn't know who but once I became aware, I processed this hidden unresolved energy that was still lodged within me. Soon I realized who it was that I needed to focus on forgiving. Before I got to work on my inner process by contemplating the issue and transmuting the energy, I received a few more indications that this work was needed.

Soon after I was having an author autograph her book for me and she wrote "Forgiveness is the Key." I asked her what that was about and she said it was just her intuition telling her to write that. On that same day, I went to hear another author speak about healing and her primary message was also about forgiveness! She miraculously healed a huge tumor through forgiveness and completely eliminated the need for surgery.

Three times in a short period of time I received the message that I was to work on forgiveness. I took this message into meditation. I just sat in my chair and contemplated what all the details were around this forgiveness and transmutation process and I asked God for help. I realized a broader perspective: that each of us is playing a role in each other's lives so that we can grow within ourselves. I thought of how overcoming all of my challenges had made me a better person, and I was grateful. Rather than having ill feelings toward anyone, I felt like each person had done me an enormous favor. It took some time to just sit and be with it, but this feeling is so real now, it has changed me in a very deep way.

Besides forgiving others, I realized I could forgive myself and every other person who had been in my life as well. Just being with that in a spirit of understanding and love healed me immensely. I felt so much lighter and have had a different perspective on life ever since.

I became aware of all the details of why I needed to forgive each person and I wrote them down. I knew forgiveness would be a process and I created an action plan. I decided to write a poem expressing my new feelings of appreciation and upliftment. The forgiveness poem goes like this:

Full Circle Love
A Poem of Forgiveness

There was a time I said to you that true love never ends
But it seemed to for a moment—you were NOT my friend
It seems that for deep healing within both of our hearts
Forgiveness is the answer; at least this is the start

So now I come to you…open to forgive
And to offer understanding so we can more fully live
To pursue our dreams and goals without scars from the past
And reconnect our friendship intending it to last

The deepest part of me has always known our souls' intention
The message I hold within me has thus far not been mentioned
We came to play a part in the drama of each other's life
To evolutionize our souls—not to patronize the strife

But more to grow and become who we truly choose to be
To live behind the veil of ignorance, but not eternally
From the expansiveness of warm and open hearts fulfilling
To a sudden contracting; leaving empty heart spaces chilling

Creating pain that surfaced in many ugly expressions
Leaving in its wake room for our life's lessons
Many years have passed now as we've both gone our own ways
I don't even know you now—for you it is the same

I feel now is the time to come together in this healing
To express and to understand what each other is feeling
As our love comes around full circle and we begin to understand
I feel that we can be close again if we lend each other a hand

Pain that heals creates within us more depth of love to care
An expansion of our true selves, a love that we can share

From this place inside my heart I come to you today
I pray that you really hear me and that God will show us the way

We are *not* victims. The highest level of our beings, our soul, creates these circumstances for our benefit. The people in our lives are experiencing the same thing: challenges from which to grow. Hopefully, as we realize this we can develop a continual nature of compassion for each other.

For myself, the application of this realization has set me free in many ways. It has also cascaded into many other realizations that make me feel more and more compassion, love, and gratitude and less and less disturbance in my heart and in my mind. I know now that in fact, there's nothing to forgive. It's all part of the divine plan and everything is perfect.

When I realized this higher wisdom it raised my awareness. I could see things from another perspective entirely. It helps me to apply unconditional love. I decided to articulate this deeper perspective inspired by God in another poem.

Nothing But Angels

The souls that walk among us
And touch our very lives
Though disguised as imperfect humans
They open up our eyes

The effect they have upon us
Is no less than divinely inspired
For these are the angels of God
From which we have inquired

As we delve inside and ask God
About life and what to do
Our answers come from All That Is
The souls of humans, too

It is these very people
On who we try out our expressions
Subjecting themselves to any behavior
Allowing for our lesson

Our lesson is the feeling we get
That tells us if we are in tune with our soul
If we express from love
Then we have reached our goal

But no matter what we do
They are here in the room with us
These angelic human creatures
Whose Divine mission we can trust

Sometimes angels have a way
Of creating undesirable drama
But we can step aside and be observers
Without creating karma

As they provide opportunity for us
To be more clear on who we are
We can hone our expressions from reactive to creative
And bless them from afar

The angels that we keep close to us
Still keep us alert all the same
They love us and they challenge us
As we play our human game

Through sharing life's experiences
Of fun and joy and laughter
We make up how we choose to live
Knowing it's evolution we're after

As we realize these people
Are angels in our lives
We feel the expression of God's love
And look beyond their disguise

As our eyes open up
And our Awareness increases
We notice we are one in spirit
Not just individual pieces

Instead of feeling the misery of illusion
We now feel the joy of unity and love
We know we are here for each other
To create the dream that life is made of

As we maintain our sense of Oneness
And express the love that we are
We thank God for the angels in our lives
And enjoy life more by far

A Global Application

It is possible that some people will beg to differ with me when we move our attention to the global situation. We see people who are seem to be entertaining ill intention and doing things like destroying the World Trade Center. We see immense corruption and medical tyranny and lies and murders. Again, a broader perspective helps relieve the issue. We can use this event to make the world a better place. It already has. Did you feel the global compassion on September 11? Wasn't it great when everyone involved put aside prejudices and exclusive belief systems to feel brotherhood and love? We noticed many acts of kindness and heroism as a result of that event. Many people learned more about themselves and what it felt like to be in that loving, caring state of consciousness.

That was its purpose. It is our choice whether we want to continue that feeling of compassion and love through forgiveness to heal our planetary conditions, or to continue allowing for oppressive and destructive energies to control our life experiences.

Now as the light comes in more fully to our awareness, we see even more. It's truly hard to fathom the level of evil that has been brought to our awareness. The crimes against children increase our compassion again. The more this truth gets revealed, the more we bond in unity and love and implement solutions.

Forgiveness can be found in our hearts. Placing our attention deep inside in quiet solitude helps us to change for the better and realize the higher order of perfection. Although we witness crimes against humanity, we know the light and love of the highest vibration wins in the end. We feel God's unconditional love and compassion for us and we get plenty to share with everyone else in our lives, too. It inspires us to take action and help wherever we can.

It is my hope and aspiration that we focus on forgiving and realize this higher perspective, both in our individual lives with everyone whose life we touch, as well as collectively so that we can generate a global feeling of love that heals the planet.

If we are open we can move from tolerance to acceptance to understanding to love. Or we can speed up the process by the realization of the purpose for our lives, forgive now, and live a life of compassion and gratitude for each other.

I am very thankful for my son, Jason, and every person, circumstance and event in my life for helping me to reach my personal evolutionary goals. I am thankful to God who resides in my heart and provides all answers. I am thankful that you would read or listen to this and contemplate the message.

Most of all, I hope you feel at peace in the presence of love now and forever.

The Evolution of Humanity

We are here at this time to break cycles. There have been cycles of abuse due to lower vibrational energies and misplacement of power. Some have tried to usurp the power of God and gain control over others. They use fear, physical attack or torture, mind control, government control, resource control, information control, inculcation and brainwashing, surveillance and data manipulation, weaponized warfare, weaponized technology, deceptive communication, and a whole host of dark powers. Their dark deeds are coming into the light of awareness now. We are using the higher intelligence of truth and love to break these cycles.

Many brave souls have come to experience abuse in order to overcome and transmute these destructive patterns of human behavior.

As truth comes to light as to the pervasiveness and horrific nature of these crimes against humanity, we feel the sad energy of deep dismay down to the core of our souls. We grieve for erring humanity. But we know our job. We know why we are here. We feel the passion and compassion of our souls. And we are strong as we tap into Divine Wisdom and seek to do God's Will.

The resurrection of humanity will come from the inherent Divine nature of our souls. Our power to overcome and break these cycles will create Heaven on Earth. The process activates our inner powers. Our DNA is activated by the necessity for change. Change is imminent. Victory is certain. It's all part of the Divine Plan and it has Purpose.

Jesus said that we can make the ethers serve the carnal self or the Divine self within. The dark forces would have us confine our awareness to a physical identity where we seek to become narcissistic and serve the physical pleasures of the body. God and soul awareness inspires us to realize our true interdimensional nature and identify with Spirit as Self and express our true Divine powers.

Our evolution is about relinquishing our selfish self and becoming the selfless self that is our true nature. We live in joy, peace, love and harmony when we express our true nature. We embody the power of love. Fear doesn't stand a chance!

We are entering a new cycle. It is a cycle of Love.

In humanity's new cycle of Love, we are evolving to our higher nature. We are evolving to higher states of consciousness. We are realizing that consciousness creates reality, and we are That Divine Consciousness—pure Eternal Essence—Spirit.

Purification and Fine Tuning

Purification allows more and more of the highest vibrational frequency to be integrated into our conscious awareness and consciousness as a whole. There is much transmutation that happens over a long period of time.

Fine tuning means having impeccable alignment and focus with Divine beingness and goals with intentions, thoughts, words, feelings, emotions, imaginings, and actions.

Intuition and inspiration allow the flow of resonant information stemming from high vibrational attunement. We are present and grounded with inner attention to the Kingdom of the Soul.

As spirit-identified beings we can clearly discern what does and does not resonate, what is or is not ours to do. At this time in our personal evolution and in the broader scope of human history, we are culminating a new re-birth of higher consciousness. We are advancing our abilities to perceive and transmit the information of pure energy, of pure love, and images of perfection.

This is no less than miraculous. Heaven on Earth is arriving!

Chapter Eight

RECIPE FOR REALITY

It's A Great Time to Be Alive!

It is so amazing to be alive right now. We are just waking up to the fact that we are creators, just like our Father-Mother God! We do have our training wheels on, though. It's a good thing. As the whole of humanity, we are not completely ready to take the helm. Why? We would not have consciously created the world as it is right now, would we? Well, we've mis-created thus far because we have had individualistic tendencies. We are one, and we have to unite in consciousness and serve the all. Luckily, God places some checks and balances into the Universal Law of Love. Any inharmony or discord is brought to light with Truth and Love. All mis-creations can be transmuted. The dream picture of Life can be made to come into alignment with the blueprint for God's Divine Plan. We cast aside the old thought patterns of being lost in illusion—the illusion of separation.

Our consciousness is changing. We are catching the Divine vision. We are casting aside Tell-A-Vision from outer sources or beings that wish to use our energy to do their bidding, and we are letting go of all of that old programming. We are laughing and loving and celebrating along the way. That's all part of the light that is coming through us.

Many people do not realize that we are one unified consciousness. But that is changing. This is the Great Awakening!

Key Ingredient: Conscious Connection to Source

Each one of us has the perfect key. We have the key to the portal of infinity! We have a direct connection to God. It is built in. "The Kingdom of Heaven is within."

Our inner connection to our Source of infinite possibilities is right inside the core of our being. Our heart center is the nexus of our soul's perception. Through attention within and conscious communion with God, we come to know our True Self. We know the kingdom of the Soul. Our true identity as Eternal Spirit is the essence of our consciousness. We are pure awareness. The forms we inhabit or create come from Spirit. They are Spirit. Spirit, or consciousness, is Light. All matter is a mass of stable Light. It is consciousness condensed to specific vibratory rates.

When we learn to master consciousness, the essence of our true selves, then we consciously create Reality. We bring Spirit into form. We build matter from light.

The Quantum Seed of Spirit is the Origin of all ideas; all intelligence. It is the land of infinite possibilities. With pure love, peace, and goodwill, we can apply the natural laws—the physics of love—and manifest anything into physical form.

We are advised by scriptures to place our heart, soul, and mind on God. We use our physical strength to build things with our hands. Our faculties are but tools of God. We attune to God and become His instruments creating from His perfect images. We must somehow realize that God is the doer, God is the originator. We are not separate from God. Our own creativity is Spirit in expression. As our identity becomes embedded in spirit our union with God is realized and expressed.

Mis-creations come from not realizing the connection to God and thinking that we are separate. We come from a space of leaning on our own discrete understanding. This self-created limitation is an illusion. It can lead to selfishness and narcissism. It is an egotistical perception of identity. It is false. This false perception is dissolved in the experience of the inner life. Inner work is necessary to cut through the ignorance of separate self-identity.

The inner life is the basis of reality. Our thoughts, imaginings, and feelings generate the energy that becomes objective reality. They are "subject" to our inner observations.

> *"Observations not only disturb what is to be measured, they create it."*
>
> Ernst Pascual Jordan
> Spanish Mathematical Physicist

We are photonic beings. Photonic synthesis is a function of consciousness. As we navigate our ship of life through the seas of consciousness, we learn to control the elements of consciousness. We are free to create.

We create images and observe them within our consciousness. We are the creator, the created, and experiencer of creation. Our mind at play results in the formation of denser vibrations that come into physical form.

Cosmic energy, chi, prana, or life energy, can be used to describe the ethers of the causal realm of consciousness. It is the substance of our creations. It contains the electromagnetic substance of light. An essential creation is a mix of thought forms, or images that are electric and feelings that are magnetic. They are married. They are one. They give birth to matter and create denser realities of objects and experiences of life.

You can stir up your emotions and use the plasma heart energy to fill a mental image based on an intentional reality choice. Or energy may come up for healing and you may process that energy through the heart receiving and transmuting the energy, then directing the energy to a new purpose by showing it the image to fulfill. The energy is directed by our will. We articulate our will through the use of clear intentions. Our images, or visions, objectify the clear intentions and we use imagination to fill in the essence of the energy and details, but we don't try to control the outcomes.

Once our formations are complete and detailed focus has held them to a point of stasis, we let go. We don't get attached to specific outcomes. Letting go and surrendering the seed of creation to the universe is where miracles of creation come from.

Once when I was consciously creating the manifestation of a lost object, after I had done my inner work imagining my object in my hands with my senses involved, I did not receive results and much time had passed. After I realized that the manifestation had not happened yet, I did a sincere letting go process. I just talked to God and said, "Well if I never get my thumb drives and lanyard back, I'll be fine anyway. Life goes on." That very night when I went to teach at a community college, months after I had originally set my intention to get my stuff back, circumstances miraculously unfolded and low and behold, I found my lanyard and two thumb drives that it contained. I *knew* it was that fact that I had truly let go because it happened *that evening!* I was so grateful.

Check Your Operating System

Your operating system is your information foundation. This foundation comes from the well that you delve into with your attention that fills up your subconscious mind, and your memory database. The scope and depth of your well of information affects the quality of your operating system.

There are three main levels of operating systems that I have observed:

1. Those who watch television.
2. Those who do independent research.
3. Those who delve into the Kingdom of the Soul.

For people who primarily receive their information from television, the scope of information is confined to the constricted flow of information that is controlled by those who own the media outlets. It is clear that the information is restricted to certain boundaries by the blatant censorship that is prevalent in the behaviors of the media's information crime squad. Certain topics are forbidden, certain messengers are banned, and information that does not conform to the mindset that is being engineered by the design of controllers is prohibited.

This scope of information is narrowly confined by very strict boundaries. Questioning is not only prohibited, it is ridiculed and discredited. There are even information police that receive large sums of money to infiltrate and obfuscate conversations. Then there are those who are hired to act as authorities that have the audacity to tell people what to believe—these are the so called "fact checkers." They don't actually check facts; they nullify information that does not come from the controllers.

There are quite a large number of people out of the whole of humanity that desire to know the actual truth behind the stories. They dig for information like anthropologists dig for ancient artifacts. They search through books, they query scientific papers and journals, they look at old newspapers and magazines, they search the internet, and they listen to other researchers. They search old newspapers. They look for stories of first-hand information from the people who are experiencers and direct observers. They gather and organize information in spreadsheets, databases, and archives online and offline. The group with this mindset uses critical thinking and discernment. The swath of information is so large, they can vet information based on connections and bigger picture synthesis. Compared to someone who only watches television, the researchers are like eagles flying above the landscape compared to a bug on the ground that see only a tiny patch of land.

There is so much information to process for the group of people who do research, that the processing of information gets refined. Discernment increases. The inner heart intelligence is activated.

There becomes a greater degree of attunement to the inner light of truth.

This leads to the third level of the information foundation: the kingdom of the soul. People who delve into the well of information that is spirit-filled and soul-centered have a deeper sense of truth. This operating system surpasses that of the conditioned mind and enters the realm of the Divine mind. The scope of awareness becomes unlimited. The mind is free. The heart intelligence is fully activated. A greater intelligence leads the seeker to the truth. Uncanny discoveries through synchronicities occur. This involves a direct connection to God – a union with the Divine mind of infinite intelligence that operates outside of time and space. Intuitive knowing is the hallmark of this attunement to Absolute Truth. When you arrive at this level of operating system, you replace belief with knowing. Minds think; hearts know.

There is no judgment regarding the information basis of a person's operating system because it is merely a progression of evolution. It all has purpose.

In truth, humanity embodies a collective consciousness. Those who have reached the broadest scope and deepest depth of consciousness serve to lift all others. The whole of humanity is evolving based on this evolutionary trend.

It's not a race or competition. We are a human family, not a human race. We are working in cooperation and unity; not opposing each other or dividing our efforts. Although there are efforts to divide and conquer us, ultimately, it can't be accomplished. Unity is an eternal fact; not just an idea or goal for the future. Our etheric essence of who we truly are is one body of light information operating with a foundational vibration of pure love. It is Self-correcting.

The light of consciousness of the awakened soul is the strongest in the electromagnetic spectrum. It cannot be entrained by lower vibrations.

As humans evolve individually, we gain empowerment and more inner light collectively. This is living love. We share consciously or automatically through the collective consciousness.

What's Really Real?

We are eternal beings of light, often referred to as soul, or spirit. We have a physical form. We can use our physical senses or our spiritual senses to access differing levels of intelligence. Our physical senses relate to us the aspects of material form. Our bodies are part of the material universe; our souls belong to the whole light universe of infinite intelligence.

Some people only give credence to the physical-material realm of reality. They identify and relate to things that can be seen, felt, touched, smelled, or tasted with the physical senses. This territory is defined with language that communicates through the corporal mind.

Others know that things that are unseen are also real. The wind blows, and we see its effects, but it has no form. Sound waves carry information to electrical devices such as radio and television, yet we don't physically see the sound waves with our naked eyes. In fact, we don't see the majority of the electromagnetic spectrum. But we do feel it in terms of vibration.

Hearts know the feeling of love. Love is a warm, soothing, and attractive vibration. Love resonates with truth.

You can't see love, though. However, it would be hard to deny the existence of love. We know that love is real. But love is one of those universal things that we all know of through our spiritual senses; through our heart and soul intelligence. It's so subtle, yet so powerful.

So what is really real? When you take a look at the physical world, you see things that are ephemeral. They come in and out of existence. A life begins, and a life ends in the physical sense. Not so with the eternal soul. Does that mean that which is eternal life is really real? Can reality be measured or defined by the length of existence?

With deeper reflection, we come to know what is real. We come to know ourselves. We begin to realize our whole being and the reason for our existence. We go further. We seek for meaning and purpose in this realm of spiritual information. We get to know our unique individual potential. Our deeper selves carry the information needed to go beyond mortal limitation and express our miraculous divine nature.

We have barely scratched the surface.

We are free, sovereign souls with unlimited power and potential. It is only through giving up or falling for deception that we become disempowered. We are destined to move beyond our physical senses, bodily identification, and the material world. There is no obstacle that we cannot overcome.

We are powerful overcomers that cannot be defined in the world of materiality, or confined by our physical senses—unless we allow it.

Love is real. We are that. And we are powerful. We can control our vibration. Our pure essence is spirit. Spirit is pure love; pure light. Light is information. It is recorded. Stored. Immutable. Accessible. We are one with it and in it.

Real Reality: Vibration and Vision

The most important aspect of Real Reality is love. It is the highest vibration. We are mastering the highest vibration by maintaining the qualities in our hearts that describe and radiate the magnetism of love. Understanding. Compassion. Forgiveness. Mercy. Grace. Unconditional love—we receive it and we give it. It is infinite. Our Source, Almighty Father God, is infinite and free.

Another important aspect of Real Reality is vision. It is the use of imagination, or creating images within. We have a laboratory where we create reality. It is consciousness. We focus attention on creative images with our conscious intentions and we get what we see. That's vision.

What's interesting is that we once believed that what we see is what we get. But after realizing that we are constantly creating, we begin to realize that what we get is what we see. It's what we see inside our imagination. We create it with our observational attention on our inner images.

If we focus most of our attention on outer reality, or things that we have already manifested, we get more of the same. But if we use our will power and consciously create by searching our souls and attuning to God's will where we catch the vision of our soul's blueprint and the divine plan, then we start to create consciously the most pristine patterns of perfection!

This is happening now. The human collective is moving into the zone of consciously creating Heaven on Earth!

It is a beautiful symphony of souls tuning in to the harmonious design of Universal Perfection. It's a cooperation of shared overlapping intentions and visions that are creating a peaceful paradise on earth where all are healthy, free, and abundant. Pristine perfection is coming into being through the purification of our consciousness.

The once muddled images of distortion are smoothing out the waters of consciousness as the collective unites morphogenic fields born of shared vibration and visions. As we each raise our vibration and clarify our divine vision from our soul's blueprint, we are raising the collective consciousness.

If anyone has not yet caught the vision, then they must free their mind. Sovereignty begins in the mind. Freedom begins in the mind. Power comes from a soul-centered being harnessing the power of the mind for conscious creations.

Inner images create outer reality. This is science. Anyone can prove it to themselves. And each one of us needs to realize this and put it into practice. That's part of mastery.

Freedom of Mind: Breaking Free of Conditioning

When we surrender our soul's sovereignty, we take up the influences of outer awareness to the extent our own inner vision and direction gets lost and we wander away from pure consciousness to the discordant vibrations brought to us through our institutional mental conditioning. They got to our minds through conditioning: a process of subtle entrainment. The entrainment impresses upon the consciousness a belief system. The belief system overrides the truth known within. It diminishes the inner knowing of the conscience. It appeals to the ego-mind. It is supported by a false sense of self. This programming feeds egos and creates narcissists. It makes false images of self that are promoted into grandeur by heightening a sense of personal power. It uses the tools of lust, greed, power, and physical domination through money and deception. It's a terrible trap!

The ideologies have grown from sores to full blown tumors of wrongful thinking and being. The methods used to lead humans astray have succeeded to the point that the group think conforming to the inculcated ideologies are thought to be the norm. The dogmas and creeds that feed the mind crap that people buy into lead to a sense of celebrity and positions of power and a false identity that binds the soul and gives over one's life energy to the bidding of evil puppeteers. Every bit of it is false. Every bit of it is detrimental to the soul of the individual and the soul of society.

Those that have fallen into these traps don't even know it. They don't know they have been captured. They don't know they are slaves. They don't know they are being controlled. They have to stay in the boxes of controlled programming, or they get emotionally triggered. They don't know peace within.

But the light is coming in. And the light will win. Scores of people are waking up daily. The cognitive dissonance comes from the soul. The inner light does not stay veiled. Instead, it illumines and resurrects to be the beacon of truth that can't be suppressed. Right now we are observing the millions of people who are standing in the truth, shouting for freedom, shining their light, and taking a stand and rocking the boat of the once effective realm of darkness and deception. The road to victory is filling up.

Calibration of Consciousness

God, the Father is the essence of All Spirit, or All That Is. As souls, we are individualized spirits. Calibration is about attunement with the highest vibration of light, the great cosmic rays of the highest intelligence that is light. In order to attune to the highest vibration of light intelligence, we get still and tune in. We settle in to the Presence. We ground our awareness into the deep still eternal moment of conscious awareness. It feels like peace. It is very soothing to the soul.

Sometimes we just do it automatically. We catch ourselves in a reverie, or just come back to the world of sensing form and have a sense of having been in the zone. It is a zone. The zone is zero point consciousness. It is always available.

Right now during our awakening process, we are catching the light of higher cosmic radiations and formulating the visions of a new reality. We catch the vision of the perfect design of God. The Architect of Perfection radiates the light into our soul, and as we attune, we are one with the illumined ideas that we submit to our subconscious minds for manifestation.

When we calibrate our consciousness to the highest God vibration, we think with our divine mind, feel with our heart full of pure love for the whole, and act from inspired passion from our soul. The power of the zone, or of being calibrated, manifests higher and higher versions of perfection.

The True Self is realized. Our spiritual nature takes precedence over our material nature. Our deeper senses come to life and become more prevalent. This is the alchemy of a rising consciousness. We receive and become higher vibrations of light.

What many have been doing over these last many years is to create an individualized spiritual practice. We have learned from each other and we have shared our processes. We process energy, transmute energy, and transcend the old versions of ourselves. Over time, the entire process has led to a complete transformation.

Ironically, the problems and challenges that are prevalent in our world right now have made our consciousness ripe for mastery, and we created them for just that. These are the catalysts for our progress for human and galactic consciousness. This alchemy of light is shifting our awareness from lower to higher dimensions. We are leaving the lower dimensions and rising to the higher dimensions through this transformation of consciousness.

Calibration of consciousness means taking control of our own mature, self-realized true identity as intelligent spirit and creating from a point of power. This means, since we are attuned to and have become one with the highest vibration of light intelligence, we create with a sense of empowerment and hold images, intentions, and visions in our imagination with the full understanding that we are the creators. We are not victims. We are awake.

My personal method of calibrating consciousness was to surrender to the Will of God on a regular basis in my meditation. I developed the faith that if I set my intention on living according to the will of God, that I would be attuned to that intelligence. I used communion. I asked a lot of questions. I would also think about any concerns I had and surrender them to God. Sometimes I would just surrender all of my thoughts, feelings, words, and actions to God and ask for transmutation and purification.

After surrender came the trust that it was so. I accepted whatever came into my life as being for the highest good. I accepted challenges as things that I need to address or process for my soul's development. It gave me a different perspective. I felt like no matter what things looked like, or whatever difficulties that I had to face, that it was for my highest good in the end. I had some real challenges, but I sure learned to manage energy better.

My inner processes made me wiser and stronger. Calibration was a daily routine. I got better at transmutation and processing. It seems that my communication and interactions with others also was honed. I knew more about what to say and what not to say. I discovered what I call "silent power" and just dealt with things within and let the energy create the outer changes that were necessary to overcome some of my challenges.

Calibration also put me in the zone to use my intentions and imagination to manifest. I know the power of attraction is very popular, but it was my inner contention that without attunement to God and the highest vibrations, we could create and attract things that might not be for the highest good. Actually, since we create all the time whether knowing or unknowingly, we have created things from the lower vibration.

For example, if we simply focus on the material plane, then we are limited to that vibration. What is physical is ephemeral. It does not last. But when we attune to the highest vibration from our soul intelligence then we manifest the higher desires that come from our soul's design and we can reach our highest potential. We tune into our passion and we become conscious creators that come from love and we naturally want to contribute to the greater good and be of service. We are more selfless than selfish.

Once we calibrate our consciousness to the highest vibration, we are free to create with infinite possibilities. We are attuned to, have access to, and are empowered by Cosmic Consciousness—the wholeness and oneness of spirit. Once calibrated, then by clarifying conscious intentions and developing detailed visions with the fervor of heartfelt feelings and powerful emotions, we consciously direct energy to manifest what we set our mind to.

Calibrated consciousness combined with imagination is changing our world and moving us toward peace, prosperity, and perfection. A precursor to this calibration is letting go of old programs and outer forms of mind control. We need to take the reins of our own minds to steer our ship of consciousness toward the greater heights of awareness and experience.

The time is now. It is time to shine. We each have the power within us. With the realization of the true Self, we are transforming the consciousness of humanity and we are emerging as the next evolutionary version of activated conscious intelligent souls. We don't need to continually dismantle the old systems and people who adhere to the lower vibrations. If they don't join us in the upward trend of evolution, they just render themselves obsolete. They do, however, have the opportunity at any time to let go of the old ways and join the bulk of humanity that is ascending to the higher realms of conscious spiritual beings of light in perfect harmony.

Choice is power. Choose to calibrate to the highest vibration, then master the light and be a conscious creator for good. Get still. Attune.

Create. "Seek ye first the kingdom of heaven, and everything else will be added to you."

Now we are set. Now we are calibrated. Let's move forward by combing the power of calibrated inspired thoughts into the powerful tool of our minds: imagination.

Imagination and Science

> "Science progresses by way of hypotheses tentatively tested and afterwards accepted or rejected according to the facts of experience. The claim that imagining creates reality needs no more consideration than is allowed by science. It proves itself in performance."
>
> Neville Goddard
> The Law and the Promise

It is absolutely fascinating to discover this power of creation that we have! This point of discovery is life-changing. The story I relayed earlier about being at the beach was my point of discovery. I know I mentioned this earlier, but by repetition, we stimulate our consciousness to remember to use our inherent skills of creation. It is good to focus on memories of your creation stories of success, too, in order to gain faith and confidence and strengthen your abilities.

One day when I was imagining that I was at the beach instead of teaching and managing a classroom full of sixth graders, many of whom were acting quite unruly at the time, when all of a sudden... circumstances changed and I found myself at the beach instead of staying at school and teaching for the remainder of the day. This was definitely "unconscious creation" but, I had done it so effectively that it had an almost immediate effect. I took notice.

Our mind precedes the reality that we find ourselves in. There is no time and no space in the zone of the eternal moment of now. What I did was go to the beach with my mind. I did this to hold my peace and not let the kids cause me any anxiety by trying to change their seemingly uncontrollable behavior. It wasn't working anyway! So, in my mind, I went to the beach and felt the sun on my face, smelled the salty air, felt the warm breeze, squished my toes into the warm sand, and I felt relaxed. My reverie only lasted for a short time. I was walking my students back from lunch. Once we arrived back, we proceeded to finish a math test, two girls got into a fight, help came, and I was sent home on workman's compensation. One girl had bit my arm and there was a slight perforation, so I was sent to get a tetanus shot. That procedure was strangely fast and then before you knew it I found myself at the beach living my vision that I had imagined as being real in my mind.

Since then, I began to use the process consciously. I also had the notion that if I calibrated my consciousness that I could manifest my soul's highest potential. For me, as an educator, that meant creating educational books, events, and programs that would teacher higher levels of consciousness. That is what I had determined was my soul's mission.

From what I am seeing, this trend toward higher consciousness is universal. Many people I know are on the path of conscious evolution. So many people are discovering consciousness ideas and tools to use to grow in awareness of self-realization and conscious comprehension and direction of energy.

Another thing I like to work with is group consciousness. I created a visioning process and I've worked with groups to manifest intentions. Sharing intentions and visions is very powerful. When we meditate together and calibrate to the zone of higher light intelligence of the whole spirit, then set intentions and make our visions detailed together, the results are predictably amazing!

Our imagination is powerful. We ARE creating our reality as we become radiant beings of pure light and pure love. This is our ascension. This is our evolution of consciousness. This is the alchemy of light. We are receiving the cosmic radiations and perfecting our world through the purification and calibration of consciousness.

Let's keep going! We are going to have many breakthroughs. We will experience much improvement through innovations. We will witness the flowering of souls reaching their highest potential. That is us. That is who we are and what we have always been meant to become. We are activated and we are actualized as full expressions of the purest essence of love.

Reality is what we make it.

Chapter Nine

BULLS-EYE FAITH

Get Your Soul Soaring!

Once you come into the knowing of your True Self, your greater
Self of soul-Spirit, you begin to soar! It's such a feeling of freedom.
It's so empowering and inspiring. It feels like the vitality of Life
has just transcended all previous levels and the shell of the old has
broken, and the star of the essential self has risen and magnified in
its intensity. It's like the spark of life within has become an eternal
flame of wisdom and wholeness.

It really is a rebirth. It really is uplifting. It is a resurrection in
consciousness!

There is a trust that is inherent in knowing the infinite intelligence
of Spirit is right inside. The reliability of this all-powerful, all-
knowing, ever-present inner Light is remarkable beyond description.

This is true empowerment: knowing and believing in your Self.

Puzzle Pieces of Life and the Big Picture

When you start reflecting on your life and all of the pieces of past
experiences, you start to grasp the purpose of each one and realize
they are all pieces in the perfect puzzle of your purposeful life.

Seeing With the Eyes of the Soul

Wherever you are on your path, your soul perception can be implemented. From the beginner to the well-seasoned spiritual practitioner, there is always a new springtime of renewed hope, wisdom, growth and change on the horizon. Creative freedom offers a canvas of infinite possibility in every moment. The zest of life is always at hand. The peace of soul is always refreshed. The infinite supply of love and light, of magnetism toward the eternal truth of being, is compelling from our very core. Enthusiasm for life and expressing one's essential nature of pure goodness from the heart is enthralling. The natural state of perfect joy and bliss beckons us onward.

The soul can see through feelings. The inner knowing is the soul's perception. It is the apprehension of the Absolute, the Eternal, and the Infinity of Being Whole. Connection is a fact that is known and sensed. Connection and wholeness is seen by the soul by feeling at One. It is union through communion with Inner Self.

To see with the eyes of the soul in the beginning, it is helpful to close the physical eyes. Change the direction of attention from outer to inner. Change the center of awareness from mind to heart. We are humble when we turn within and ask. Asking questions with full faith in receiving a response is a mark of an awakened soul. An awakened soul is one who identifies as an eternal spirit rather than a mortal physical body.

This identity transformation is not complete overnight. It takes practice. Regular practice. It takes time to recognize and develop the language of the soul. Yet, it is natural, quick, and easy to tune in.

Seeing through the eyes of the soul is best accomplished by giving time and space a break. Stop the perception of time by being still. Halt the perception of space by centered awareness. The zero point is in the center of being.

Going into the zero point state of consciousness is like entering a thick forest and sitting down in the middle of it. Only instead of a place, it is a state of being. It is where the conscious meets the subconscious and the superconscious minds. It is a state of neutrality. It is a clear, free perspective. It is a state of "not knowing" anything to reach the state of "All-Knowing" everything. It is the access of infinite information.

It sounds paradoxical because it is. Life is paradoxical. But paradox is reconciled in the state of consciousness where we apprehend the Absolute with soul perception through the heart.

We feel innocent and trusting, like a child in this state of consciousness. We know there is something greater. It is a greater intelligence. We form our union with the Absolute by communion. Meditation and prayer are forms of deep communion. Self-reflection, contemplation, and imagination all tap the zero point field of infinite consciousness.

With the eyes of the soul, we can "see" or comprehend the light—the infinite light of creation, the pure love of the Creator, and Absolute Truth replete with all the wisdom of the ages.

Through constant contact and communion, identity continues to shift. Enlightenment and empowerment grow and grow. Sometimes it is so subtle, progress is hardly noticeable. However, once looking back on the former way of being remarkable progress becomes evident.

The process of amalgamation of soul and spirit has been slowly taking place. It's not that there was any separation; it is identity and perception that is changing. It's a transference of self-awareness. This is huge!

Imagine being confined to a physical, mortal, limited identity with issues of self-esteem and self-worth. Then retreating to the chrysalis of inner awareness only to emerge a limitless being of Eternal Light! Those who let in and honor the Light of Truth walk in integrity. We become the living Truth. That's how we blend with spirit—seeking and living the Truth.

Our souls perceive the Truth through Love. Loving God; loving the center of Self, loving the Light within. You can call it anything you like that resonates with you. It IS the Absolute. It IS the essential nature of all life. It IS the Source of all life. It is the Alpha of idea and the Omega of energy where manifestations of ideas return, only to become available for another creation. It is the manifest and the unmanifest. It is the possibility and the manifestation. It is the particle and the wave. It is Source and Substance. It is thought and feeling.

We all see with the soul. We all have soul perceptions. Our impetus is to recognize these perceptions, value them, live by them, and develop our abilities of and through the soul-Spirit that we are.

As the field of awareness increases through soul-Spirit communion, empowerment escalates. Inner knowing with certainty builds trust in intuitive perceptions. Discernment proliferates. A sense of power from within is felt. Inner strength is from the Light of Truth that is lived. A person of integrity is much stronger and markedly more powerful that one who is deceitful or selfish or prideful.

Since Truth is based in Love, they grow together. A person of integrity knows wholeness. Compassion, love, mercy, and grace compel kindness and helpfulness. There is sincere forgiveness for those who "know not what they do" because the process of increasing awareness of the whole can see the entire process of evolution. We don't condemn those who are at different stages. We have been at each stage ourselves. We have missed the mark along the way. We cast no stones of judgment. However, we know we must stand for the needs and rights of others with the strength of Being that we have developed.

With the wisdom of the soul garnered by inner work and self-development, we seek solutions that are for the highest good of all. We are all changing in this regard (good work!), and we are changing our world.

Conducting Energy from the King of Love

Our Inner Light is a Source of infinite energy. By giving the Inner Spark of Light that is at the core of our being Love, we generate, emanate, and radiate this energy. Through will power and intention, we increase its intensity. We can amplify and share the energy.

Identify with the light, the Christ of God. Identify through affirmations. Identify through realization of this truth. Wield the Light!!! Recognize that power within and use it to full capacity. We are being empowered in this way at this time.

Completely let go of any fear or unbelief. Feeling is believing, nay, it is more! Being One with Truth is certain knowing. We can practice using our power. Since we are grounded in Love, there can be no misuse of energy. We always are grounded in Peace and Goodwill. There is NO POWER that is sustainable without Peace and Goodwill.

The King of Love is the highest vibration of Being. Identify with Pure Love through affirmations, realization, and diving deep into the heart and soul of your essential nature. Dissolve any sense of low self-worth. There is nothing greater than the essence of Absolute Essential Eternal Self that is known. We learn to operate through this consciousness through expression. Expression comes in the form of creativity, giving, and helpfulness.

Affirmations and the Subconscious Mind

We are reprogramming our subconscious minds to undo and unlearn the part of our minds that have been usurped to manifest others' visions and agendas. The subconscious mind is that part of consciousness that hold the patterns for the creation of reality. In our awakening, we are controlling our own subconscious mind.

The subconscious mind primarily gets programmed in two distinct ways: through repetition and deep emotions.

Those that employ mind control techniques know this. For example, commercials will pull at your heart strings with emotion evoking scenes, and then they will tell you to buy something. After that, they show you scenes of happiness and joy as if the thing they are selling will make that happen. Then they repeat those commercials over and over again. This is a setup. You unconsciously create from that pattern.

To reverse this condition, stop watching commercials. I stopped watching television or listening to radio stations with commercials a long time ago. I really sense the mental freedom within myself. This understanding goes a long way in producing inner peace and freedom.

Affirmations are super important to reverse and implant new programs. They are essential in regaining sovereignty of mind. I use affirmations every day. In the morning I read some spiritual literature. Then I pick out some important points that I want to implant in my subconscious mind. Some examples are: "I am pure love and wisdom doing God's will." "The infinite intelligence within me guides me and solves all of my problems." "Thank you, God for another perfect day. Thank you for every breath I take." "I am peaceful and poised in every moment and I am guided to make the highest choices."

Affirmations also work well to manifest intentions. Put everything in the now moment with gratitude. "Thank you, God, for blessing the children I work with." "I'm so grateful for the blessings of peace." Embedding affirmations with gratitude increases the supply of anything we are grateful for.

Feeling deeply and sincerely from the heart also embeds the subconscious mind to activate the law of infinite supply. Once when I didn't have much money, I took what little I had, some cash and a small check, and I held my hands over it and held my mental focus, as I poured love and gratitude energy from my heart and through my hands for what I had and gave thanks. The next day I received more cash and a bigger check!

Sleep Working

Another way to employ the subconscious mind is repeating affirmations while going to sleep. "The infinite intelligence within me brings me perfect health. I am healthy, strong, and energetic." "My inner source of wisdom knows the solution to…" "I feel so wonderful! I'm so thankful that ….has occurred in my life."

A friend of mine went to sleep contemplating a problem with

wiring on his old truck that he couldn't figure out. He tried one thing after another, but nothing had worked. He woke up super early in the morning and the perfect solution was presented to his mind. He went out and did what was presented and everything worked again on his truck.

Navigating through the Great Awakening

During the worst cataclysm we might express a deeper and greater part of our Self than we have ever known. We might do something heroic. We may do something that is super kind and selfless. Troubles often activate latent soul abilities. Horrible things might happen with amazing miraculous outcomes in their wake—miracles born of love and compassion. It's in each one of us.

There is no sense of lack with True Self-awareness. There is no limitation. All the old programs that constrain the power of the soul are GONE! Say goodbye once and for all with inner will power to all that may try to control or restrict your true power!

Centered in Source individuals have no need for drama. Drama is just the result of unconscious individuals trying to get energy from the outside instead of inside by stealing it from other people. Unconscious people don't even realize why they act the way they do. They don't understand their need for attention. Attention within fulfills their needs. But if they don't know any better, they may seek outer attention. Sometimes it gets so intense that they mark their character through expressions of egotistical or narcissistic words and actions. To higher vibrational beings, the low vibration of an unconscious person feels uncomfortable or dissonant.

Boundaries can coincide with unconditional love to address energy thieves. In fact, one of the lessons on the road to higher consciousness is the ability to address issues with clear communication of boundaries. Self-love and self-protection is a necessary skill for soul advancement.

We are becoming the authority of our own energy fields. We

are learning to control our vibrations with our thoughts. We are mastering vibration also by lifting up our sense of joy, peace, and happiness when things in life happen that bring us down. We are the overseers of our own consciousness. During the transformational process, it takes learning, practice, and vigilance.

Resurrection Tools to Raise Vibration

Once we set our intention to keep our vibration high, we tend to notice if it dips. There are many tools we are learning and practicing to keep our vibration at higher levels. Several of the many things we can do to lift our vibration include:

- Gratitude – Switch the focus of attention on something or someone you are grateful for. Hold the focus and feel the gratitude deeply and sincerely. Even make a mental list of current blessings.
- Surrender - Ask for help, then let go and let God. Release the concern to the universe and have faith. The help always comes!
- Love – Focus on someone you love and send them that love. Transmit light.
- Focus on an Eternal Truth – God loves you!
- Transmute – Consciously transmute the energy with compassion, motherly nurturing love, or the violet flame. Compassion for your self is essential. Compassion for others is equally important.
- Positivity – Think positive thoughts or elicit inspired ideas.
- Create – Imagine creating with your favorite personal form of creative expression.
- Lift the load – Do a chore or something for someone you know to lighten their load of responsibilities.
- Brighten someone's day – Write a note of appreciation and give it to warm the heart of someone. You could speak kind

words, too, but the written word may be a keepsake that they can re-read.

- Sing or listen to uplifting music – Hold the feeling of praise, love, and gratitude while singing a soulful song. Use it to anchor in the highest God vibration of the pure love of God.

All-Powerful Peaceful Presence Perceived by the Soul

Peace is power. Peace is perceiving the zero point state of consciousness. Inner peace creates a slate of reflection for the higher intelligence to convey images of wisdom and perfection. The details of the needed guidance can be gained by reading the Blueprint of the Soul. The Divine Plan can be accessed to gain awareness of the bigger picture of life that reveals the purity, perfection, and purpose of life.

Peace is the first and foremost gift of soul perception. It is the door to everything. It is the path of higher, broader, and deeper perceptions. The mind can never access the subtle information that the soul can perceive. But when our house is in order, the mind can serve the soul and use its magnificent wise perceptions.

The depth of Peace increases as the inner world is developed through attention and love. We are souls and our true essence is peace. Knowing peace is knowing ourselves—our True essential eternal Self.

The wealth of Self is found within. The power of peace is found within. It is the Kingdom of Heaven; the Kingdom of the Soul. Peace feeds our whole being with Love. We sense our connection and feel very loved when we settle into this inner peace. We literally send others our energy when we pray for them or think of them with love, compassion, and concern. There is no time or space in this zero point. People we care about receive the blessings of our love through the radiance of our thoughts and attention to them.

Our natural connection is the Oneness that we know and use consciously as we awaken to our soul identity and knowledge of our soul power.

Yes, our thoughts are VERY powerful. We are using them constantly to send out radiant energy. The photonic power of our thoughts hit the mark according to the direction our attention. We know that wherever our attention goes, our energy flows. It cannot be stated too often how important it is to consciously direct our attention and maintain a high vibration. Our energy is LOVE at its highest vibration. *Giving attention is giving love.*

"Hold your peace" means to stay tuned to that peaceful presence that emanates from within. Peace is the foundation of union. Union is the natural powerful bond of love. Magnetic love is radiant energy.

Focusing on Patterns of Perfection Instead of Appearances

We are creators. We are becoming conscious creators. Traditionally, we have been focusing more attention on the outside, looking toward the world of appearances. Appearances are what we have called reality. Appearances have largely been thought of as physical or material reality. What appears to be solid form has been determined to be mostly space.

Essentially everything is light. Light is what emanates from consciousness. Every so called solid object is just a mass of stable light. And most of its mass is empty space! We are the projectors of the light that becomes matter.

Our understanding of the process of how consciousness creates physicality is a new idea on the horizon of human consciousness. We are really, as a whole, just starting to get it. And once we get it, it takes a whole fundamental shift on how we process energy from the essence of our being—the conscious light energy that we are.

What is cosmic consciousness? It is the simultaneous awareness of everything. What is Christ consciousness? It is the awareness of Self as Light in a unified field of Love. What is God consciousness? It is the awareness of the union of the whole infinite field of light at the zero point of Absolute Eternal Essence.

Unity consciousness signifies an operating system stemming

from inner awareness of Source and Substance. It is the reconciliation of paradox, the union of opposites. Truth is the apex of polarity, like the tip of a sword. The edges are divided, but the tip is the union of the sides.

At the realization of unity, there is a comprehension of inherent design. In the seed of the soul is the design of its perfection. There is a blueprint that drives the soul into perfect expression. As the soul catches the vision of its perfection, the mind is mastered. The vision of perfection is held in focus.

Appearances lose their value. Appearances are expressions, or radiations of the past. It is in the center of Being that creation takes place. In order to reflect the perfect design contained in the inner spark that holds the original thought seed pattern of perfection, we need only to get still and silent and reflect. We are on the "receiving" end of the vision of perfection. Once we catch it, we hold our focus and embellish the essence of it with images and feelings.

When we realize how to utilize causal consciousness, we learn to create consciously through the process of receptivity, intention, and visioning. We get attuned through love and surrender.

We master our minds by focusing on our inner peaceful center, accessing the blueprint or patterns of perfection held within our soul, and by using concentration to bring those patterns into being. We don't just stop with the vision, of course. But we get very clear and use will power and the energy that is in motion in our hearts (emotion) to unite and form the new seed of reality.

During this time of transformation, we have to become conscious, independent thinkers. We benefit and accelerate our competence as creators the more we shift our attention from outer appearances to the designs of perfection. Our attention is constantly being drawn into technology, entertainment, outer chatter and rhetoric, and entities and energies that seek to gain our energy through capturing our attention. We need to recognize what is happening and gain control of ourselves, starting with the control of our attention.

The world of appearances is a temporary mirage, despite how much credence has been given to it in the past. It is SO yesterday!

Really, it is a former creation. You can change the creation by manipulating the outer world. You change the world of creation by mastering the mind, its direction of attention, and the vibration of emotional energy. Stillness is the key. Inner peace is the key to outer peace.

We are overcoming victim consciousness. We are waking up to our powers. We are not always pleased or amused at what has been created. We are quite appalled and dismayed at much of it. But, the good news is: We can identify and recognize Truth. Centered in the essence of Love, we embody and know Truth. Appearances, like so much worn out energy, dissolve. We know that energy can be transmuted and transformed. We just transcend our former identity and perspective and see the whole bigger picture with the perception of the soul. The soul is our home, our true identity, and our union with the whole Self.

We come to know, trust, and believe in our True Self.

The Integrity Model of Consciousness

The Integrity model of consciousness consists in the four pillars of Self-Actualization. Self-actualization is the perfect unfolding of the potential within the soul-seed. This perfect realization and expression of unique soul potential is mastered by (1) Knowing your True Self, (2) Being True to the inner knowing of Truth within the heart and soul of Self, (3) Being the expression of the authentic True Self, and (4) Believing in the strength, power, talents, gifts, attributes and purpose of the True Self.

In short, the foundation of the Integrity Model of Consciousness is built from these four tenets:

- <u>Know</u> Thy True Self
- <u>Be True</u> to Thy True Self

- Be Thy <u>Authentic</u> True Self
- <u>Believe in</u> Thy True Self

Every soul has a unique purpose that is fulfilled by activating the potential within. Inner work is involved in the accessing and activation of pure soul potential. Inner work is taking time and attention to go within and access information. Information is Truth. Information is Light. Science has already determined that the universe is made up of "mind stuff". Mind stuff is thought. Ideas, information, and truth—all form the light of consciousness.

Each soul is a powerful, highly valuable, and packed with individual potential that is a fractal of infinite intelligence.

Attention is required for activation. Attention within. Attention to the seed that contains the blueprint for perfection. Attention to the information that will be revealed through heartfelt communion. Questions, curiosity about Self, love of True Self, Love of Truth, Love of God and others: all of these things bring one to the utterly fascinating world of True Self Realization and Expression.

We know and embody the truth of who we are through expression. We get our inherent feeling of value, or intrinsic value, from doing the right thing, doing the best thing, or creating something beautiful to give the world.

Intrinsic value is really important. It has not been stressed enough in education or society as a whole. It had been downplayed as we focused our identity on outer appearances of the physical body or material possessions. But now it's time for change. Now it's time to realize our True Self-Worth. We ARE inherently worthy! We are priceless! We are each an integral, needed, valued, and appreciated part of the whole.

We are responsible and accountable. We are singular and sovereign. We are individual and powerful. We are conscious and intentional. That's the new way of being. That's what we are becoming. Our transformation, individually and collectively, is well on its way.

A good practice during these transformative times is just to take a moment of self-reflection and think of how valuable we are.

Everything we think, say, do and feel has an immense effect in our world. More than we used to realize. Self-reflect and focus on this fact of individual value. We don't need to dwell on shortcomings or past mistakes. These are just stepping stones to self-mastery. Some of our greatest lessons have come from our mistakes. We have all missed the mark of perfection. That's ok. We just don't give up. We just don't stop trying to access our Source of power and perfection.

Every experience has its value. Every circumstance, event, and relationship has its purpose. There is only good. Self-reflection finds the blessing and the purpose by knowing it is there and determining to find it. Our True Self knows what it is. We are in communion in our inner world. We have access to the information we need. Our Self is the Source of all information.

Self-worth is built by a determination to live according the Integrity Model of Consciousness. Its aim is toward perfection. Bulls-Eye Faith means you believe in your Eternal Essence of Soul Light to guide you and keep you moving toward your ultimate expression of perfection. When we get it right and do what is right or express a great quality of being, we are assured from within our conscience the inner feeling of personal value. It is deep and true. It cannot be mistaken.

Just think for a moment on a time you helped someone out. Inside you KNEW it was good and right. You felt good about yourself. It is a natural feeling and it builds strength of character. It is morally right. It is ethically right. It feels deeply good to express goodness. Goodwill is God's will.

What if the goals of people around the world shifted to feeling good about being good, helpful and giving from the old paradigm of personal gain and self-preservation? That's what the evolving humanity is up to in this transformation of consciousness. Conscious people are givers.

Magnify Only the Good

Outer appearances can feel in tune with Truth when they are whole, peaceful, beautiful, and life renewing. Nature is a good place to be to get centered in peace and harmonious vibrations that are in tune with the whole.

If an outer vision vexes the spirit because it seems inharmonious, we can create an inner vision overlay based on an image of perfection, or a perfect solution. Catch and create a vision of perfection and consciously replace the appearance mentally with a better image. I call this "Vision Lifting". Whether we are looking outside at appearances or inside at an image, we are beholding a vision.

We don't have to accept or buy into appearances or suggestions that are less than perfect. We have the ability to consciously create a new reality, or appearance. Now that we are becoming conscious, that is our responsibility. We have the ability to respond to imperfection with the solution or with patterns of perfection that we can replace them with. It may take practice, but the results are worth it!

Our mental images, or our imagination, create our reality. With focus and feeling united, we are learning to be better at creating the outer world. We are not victims of our creations—we are masters in the making!

Focus Magnifies Images and Brings them Into Form

In order to magnify and bring patterns of perfection into form, we need to learn and practice concentration. Concentration requires stillness. We need to learn to be still and focus our mental attention on images that we CHOOSE to create. In order to be effective, we need to HOLD the vision, dive into it, and create the emotional energy vibration that comes with it.

We become one with the vision through focused inner attention. We are not looking *at* the image of creation; we are *in* the image of creation. We can feel the essence of the circumstance or experience we are creating consciously.

Contrary to former popular belief, our mind does not travel according to our body, but our body travels according to our mind. We are going to realize the impact of this power the more we understand and practice it.

Our minds have been manipulated, co-opted, and directed by social engineering. We need to recognize this fact and exit the system of mind control. The best way to exit is to get back to Self. As long as we are letting others or outer circumstances determine the direction of our attention and our thoughts, we are being controlled rather than being in control.

Stepping out of the milieu of the controlled population has significant value by freeing the mind to suit higher purposes. Stepping out just has to do with getting time alone, or getting time in nature.

Quiet reflection is necessary for freedom.

In fact, complete control of the mental faculty is the *foundation* of freedom. Since your body and physical reality follows the mind, free your mind and your whole being will be free.

Neville Goddard tells us his story. He was drafted into military service. He did not want to be there. He asked his superior for a discharge. He was turned down. At night he went to sleep imagining that he was at home in his own bed in his apartment in New York. About nine days later, his superior came to him with paperwork to sign for an honorable discharge. He used the power of a free mind. Reality complies.

You can learn more about Neville Goddard by reading his books *The Law and the Promise*, and *The Power of Awareness* or by looking up the audio recordings of his lectures on YouTube. He tells us that the power of imagination is scientific: you can prove it to yourself through application.

Know Your True Self

Get centered in peace. Feel the essence of your own being. Know your inherent worth. Just go into your own heart and examine how you feel. Check out what is foremost in your mind. Know your thoughts and feelings and what makes you tick. Go deeper and deeper. Go within often. Commune with God. When you have heart to heart talks with God, then you know what it feels like to be sincere. You can learn to be honest with yourself. That's how you really get to know yourself.

Take time for inner processing of emotions, thoughts, and impressions you get from life. You have a depth of perception within your soul. You can delve deep within and reach into God's wisdom. You have unlimited resources inside that is part of your True Self.

Take notice about what interests you. Discover your passion. Get clear about your purpose. Contemplate the things that really stir your soul. It is natural to be driven toward things that arouse your curiosity. The magnetism you feel toward something leads you toward your passion. Pay attention to the level of intensity of your feelings. Some things might just seem boring or so-so. Other things lift your spirit and bring you joy. Some things might even anger you, and that might be something you want to put your life energy into to make things better.

Your True Self is a soul with deep heart intelligence. This is a place where you can direct your mind and expand your consciousness. When you take the time to be by yourself for self-discovery, you get inspired. You are amazing! And you are a gift to our world.

Be True to Your True Self

Your True Self has a voice. It's called your conscience. Listen to it. Follow it without fail. Inner strength will increase. You will feel the power of the Inner Light built by living with integrity.

Don't do what you know is wrong. Don't get persuaded to do

something you don't want to do. Follow your own counsel within. Don't let others coerce you or override your God-given free will choice.

Love your Self. Stand up for your Self. Speak up for what you believe is right.

Take care of your needs. Protect your rights.

Stand strong and firm. The Light within is powerful.

If you fall down, get back up again. If you make a mistake, then vow to do better. If you get depressed, take time to listen to the wisdom of your soul.

Be your Authentic True Self

You are who you are on the inside. You don't have to make any pretentions or appearances of being somebody you are not. Just be you. Don't try to be like anyone else. Take pride in being unique.

Love and accept yourself just the way you are. As you move through life you will discover all of your inner gifts and heavenly treasures. They always show up at the perfect time.

Be in the moment and honestly speak your true feelings with gentle honesty. If you don't know what to say, just ask God. He will always show you the way.

Believe in Your True Self

God planted in your soul a wealth of treasure. Your personal seed contains such unique qualities and gifts that there could be no possible duplication. Your magnificence shines like the brightest star-like jewel that has the potential of a thousand suns! Once you know your True Self, you can have perfect faith that in partnership with God you can express all that you have within you. Know that you can do anything, and you can. Believe in your True Self because as you shine your God qualities and express your unique creativity, you will realize your self-worth comes from within. Your worth comes directly from your Creator who always has you in His heart and encompasses you within his arms of love. His messenger angels surround and protect you. With no fear and perfect faith, you have all you need to believe in yourself.

Causal Consciousness

Your soul is refined through education and contemplation of new spiritual wisdom. You are clearly on an upward journey. The path is made clear. A shift has been made from solely outward flowing attention and energy to a new pattern of inward attention and flow of energy. This cultivates the soul and your true identity becomes evident.

The power that is accessed is tempered by the essence of the inner world. It is comprised of the feeling of deep peace. It is magnetized by the sense of self that is pure love. The True Self-awareness brings the soul into the resonance of Spirit. From this resonance comes the gift of mastery. It is the overcoming of the small sense of self into the realization of the Greater Self.

The Greater Self knows itself as the cause of reality. It is on the throne of consciousness. It is the Oneness with the God vibration. Lower vibrations are left behind. There is a process of purification and transmutation that stabilizes and anchors in this new level of higher consciousness.

The mind is free. You create from visions of your ideal reality. You live in your created world of peace and freedom. You intuitively know your soul's blueprint and what you are going to accomplish as your life's mission.

You see the inner light. You receive the light while focusing attention within. The light from God, the Father, or Source is infinite and free. There is a depth of wealth—a wealth of Truth including ideas and inspiration. It is effervescent. It is the essence of joy and happiness and beauty and creativity.

Dwelling in peace, you retain a sense of pure love vibration. You absorb the essence of tranquility and beauty, and your being rejoices in the eternal moment of now. There's no sense of time or space. This is the point of creation. You know yourself as the cause of created reality.

Your path to Home is well known. It is the zero point consciousness where you are consciously creating reality. You have consciously calibrated your consciousness by matching your vision and vibration with the Divine Mind of the Greater Self.

Perceive the inner. The inner becomes the vastness of the absolute peace. The outer reality manifests from the center of being.

All tools and processes of a consciously calibrated consciousness conspire with the universe to create the synchronicities, opportunities, experiences, blessings, and miracles that arise as the heart's desires. The pristine patterns of perfection are realized and articulated through will power and stated intentions, and become manifest in perfect universal harmony through loving cooperation with other attuned souls.

All glory to God as souls flower into their highest potential of ideal expression! Each unique soul is essential to the garden of love, peace, and goodwill that comprises Heaven on Earth.

Create a Vision and Start Where You Are

It's time to really follow your heart. It's time to really love your Self! Get real within yourself. Explore your feelings, interests, talents, gifts, and passions. Take some time to journal. No matter where you are in life, you have someplace to grow.

Your soul knows where you are. You soul knows where you are going. If you would like assistance with the inner work of exploring your soul, you can get the *Bulls-Eye Faith Inner Work Book.* (Check www.smile4love.com for availability.)

Reflect often on your True Self and you will be directed and inspired to move forward. You will be moved to release things that have spent their season. You will be inspired to bring new springtime treasures of new beginnings or improvements to what you already have. You can assess the different areas of your life through introspection. You can make higher level decisions about what to do or how to handle things.

Every day things change. Life changes. Staying clear within yourself helps you to go with the flow and also to make much progress. Moving forward may mean accomplishing things that your soul has set for you to do. Clarity and inspiration are great gifts from your soul. They are always available.

After self-reflection, set your conscious intentions. Spend time daydreaming. Give your attention to your dreams. Live within them for a time. Expand your mind and engage your senses to feel all of the sensations of living your dreams come true.

You are mastering your life energy. You have mastered vision and vibration. There is nothing you can't overcome. There is nothing that you can't accomplish.

You are clearly on a path of transformation. Already you can see you have been prepared for this moment in time. This is really your time to shine!

Chapter Ten

THE ALCHEMY OF LOVE

When humans understand how love transforms,
distorted perceptions are no more...

The Transformation of Consciousness

Have you ever tried to put a genie back into a bottle? How about putting something large and unwieldy back into its package? Maybe like a tent or sleeping bag back into its original bag? It's sometimes difficult. But that's what it is like for me to attempt to explain the process of transformation: the soul's amalgamation with Spirit. The Good News is that this amalgamation is what happens naturally as our soul essence expands into the Whole of Spirit.

It all starts with the Inner Spark. This inner spark, the intelligence of awareness within is our identity. But we don't know that at first. We come into these bodies and get conditioned by materialistic values and socialized programming. Our natural sense of essence that we are born with essentially gets stuffed into the bag of body awareness. Our true sense of Self diminishes. We buy into limitations.

Eben Alexander puts it rather succinctly. This is a quote from his book, Proof of Heaven: "We are free; but we are free beings hemmed all around by an environment conspiring to make us feel that we are not free."

The moment we begin to point our attention within, we commence traveling on the road to Freedom. Inner awareness leads us to the Source and Substance of our BEing. We perceive our own essence. We break free of limitations. We are freed from victimhood, because within is the realm of cause.

Once within, we even escape our own minds eventually. We become aware of the Absolute. The Absolute is the Essence of Everything. It is undivided Presence. Some call this Spirit. Some call this God. Some call this love. Some see it as substance. But the seeing varies. It depends on how deep you go.

Regular practice of going within, (reflection, meditation, contemplation, concentration, etc.) increases the scope and depth of consciousness. This expands awareness. Identity shifts. Awareness of self ("self-concept") is synonymous with identity.

When an individual does not go within, they tend to identify with the body and external things. An ego is built this way. Intelligence is limited by defining, confining, and conforming. Materiality is the sole substance. Wholeness is replaced by separation and compartmentalization. It's off track. There is no center. It's the way of the Prodigal Child.

But once a decision is made to go within and be honest with one's Self and feelings, awareness expands and identity shifts. The Divine Spark gets attention. The attention "fuels the fire" so to speak. Illumination begins. The Kingdom of Heaven is entered. The Kingdom of the Soul is Heaven—the infinite eternal context of Being.

The process of going in to the world of spirit and going back out into the world of form, or physicality and materiality, is like weaving a tapestry. Connection is realized. The cause and connection of thoughts and feelings and self-concept becomes known to be the source and substance of experience. Manifestation of outer experiences and the world at large empowers the awakening soul.

Who knew such potential was hidden like a treasure right within? Who knew what miracles would unfold? Who knew what level of discernment could be developed? Who knew what it would be like to activate powerful perceptions? And who knew the Absolute power of imagination without limitation?

Genius is born as this discovery takes place. It's always been there, waiting to be discovered. The spark of genius was just waiting for the eye of attention to ignite its activation. When I was teaching, I always reminded my students that they were all geniuses. I meant it because I knew it. I'm sure those seeds that have been planted are growing now. I still send those souls my love.

Throughout this process of going within and expressing in the material world, the tapestry of life unfolds. The soul, knowing its eternal essence, expands its awareness and deepens its perception.

Resonant souls with like intentions are connected by vibration and frequency. The general population is affected by every soul that awakens to their True Identity. The True Identity is the Light of Absolute Truth: the non-dual spark of the heart. And thus, has Heart Intelligence been born in Humanity.

Peace is the result of experiencing the Essence of Presence. As one becomes this peaceful presence, the genius comes out of the bottle of the body. The whole Spirit of Humanity has evolved.

Never mind those who decide not to evolve. Either they will move to another place of matching frequency, or their essence will dissolve if they refuse to match the vibrational frequency of the now evolved humanity and planet Earth. The Love Vibration is stabilizing. The contrast of the lower intelligence is becoming evident, and I have to say, somewhat amusing.

Let's pray for all to catch up and wake up. All it takes is a commitment to Truth. All it takes is a purified, caring heart. All it takes is a bit of humility to take in some new information. As we radiate our essence of love, we are tuning forks to assist everyone who wishes to partake in this vibration. The invitation is extended to all. Grace, mercy, and forgiveness are part and parcel of this new vibration. All it takes is for a soul to say: "Yes!"

Inside, where the alchemy of love is taking place, each soul expands to know the context of Whole Intelligence. You may relate to it as the Holy Spirit of Truth. Light. Consciousness. Substance. Cause.

The transformation of consciousness is marked by a shift from linear living and perception to contextual, or nonlinear, living and perception. Radiance of the soul is felt as joy and genius expression. Heart intelligence is the hallmark of the new race of humanity.

Celebration is in order. However, we have work to do. We have to use our powers to clean up the past. We need to dissolve outdated institutions. We need to relieve those who abuse their power of duties when they are out of integrity. And we need to listen within to know who is appointed to take their place. We need to use our strength and stand up for what is right.

In the end, we will create a peaceful world where all prosper and express their genius. In the field of joy and love, we live, move and have our being. We are creating a new environmental context. We know that unity of purpose inspires cooperation. Diversity is accepted. Love has no bounds. It IS the intelligence of the heart. It IS the result of soul amalgamating with spirit.

We are one with the Absolute now. We know the essence of Presence. The genius is out of the body bottle, and it's NOT going back in.

Allow. Flow. Trust, and BE. You are FREE!

Energy Conversion

Energy is neither created nor destroyed, but within our consciousness we can change its form. We do it when we cry. We are releasing energy. We do it when we think. We give energy form. We are constantly converting energy.

One interesting perspective is to treat the energy as an intelligent entity. We can acknowledge energy as intelligent information with purpose, and then we can convert the energy from one purpose to another. We are constantly addressing the energy that comes to or through our energy field in everyday life.

Our inner processing can be developed as we learn to better understand our life energy and master our destiny.

Order of operations: God-Self-Others-God

Here is an explanation that will serve as an overview of the way to process energy from resistance (any negative energy, thought, or emotion), through acceptance, and into love. Love is Source Energy that can then be transformed into anything that we would like to create to form our reality that matches our highest good.

As we process, we can begin by feeling and sensing God's unconditional love for us. To do this, just focus your attention on God and ask to feel His love. Breathe and relax and the feeling will come. It will feel like you're being relieved of something. You will begin to feel lighter. You may notice tingling in your body or a warm feeling in your heart. A smile may come across your face. You may feel touched by God by a gentle breeze or by hearing some words in a song that you sense and intuitively know as coming from God. You may feel God's presence in any number of ways. As you get present with the love of God, just purposefully being on the receiving end of love, you relax at the deepest level and feel inner peace. Now it is time for the next step.

Look at yourself. As you focus your attention on yourself, on how you are, on how your life is, do it with an attitude of acceptance. Those things that bother you about yourself, the ones you persistently beat yourself up for, stop and say to yourself: "It's ok. I am just fine just the way I am. Ok, this is the way I am in this moment. There's a reason for it and I will find the blessing in it, the wisdom. And for that, I will love it. I will love me and I will love my life. I am in the perfect process of life, and though already perfect and loved just the way I am, I will get even better."

Think of other people that you know that you may have some resistance to. Everybody has a reason for being the way they are and thinking and believing the way they do. By accepting and loving them just the way they are, it changes the energy dynamics within your relationship with them. It opens the flow of love. Find something to love in everyone.

Instead of wondering or expecting what others think of you or feel about you, try just loving *them* unconditionally and see what happens. Speak your truth honestly and openly. Be authentic. Love yourself. Know that God loves you always just the way you are. When fulfillment comes from within, there is nothing we need from without, and that includes other people. When we go inside and connect with God, our cups runneth over. We have an abundance of love to share. We don't need to feel like we need anything from the outside; from others. We become the source of love, and they will naturally feel an affinity for us for the love and the light we bring to the experience of us in the moment.

Transformation of Energy

Another way you can help, if you're not doing it already, has to do with the transformation of energy. We can use our minds and hearts to internally process the energy. Like a sculptor, we can remold it. We can give it a new vision and a new purpose. We can change it with the power of love.

I realize we have some negative energy that is playing itself out on this planet, but we *can, as individuals,* transform the energy now and help create peace.

We are all part of the same spiritual intelligent energy system. We share thoughts as we exchange energy, whether we are conscious of it or not. The morphogenic field is our unified energy field from which we all contribute and we all derive conscious energy from. This fact has many implications, but mostly we can use it to our advantage if we wish to make positive global changes.

First, when we realize we are a dynamic integrative part of the same whole, we realize we have a responsibility in terms of what we create with our energy.

The way to create peace on earth is for each person to take any negative energy that comes into their personal space and transform it into love with a conscious process. Transform the energy into love by feeling compassion for humanity. Then consciously send that love with an intention and vision to transmit, and see the light reaching people, places, or circumstances.

This means in every personal relationship or circumstance, when negative energy comes up from within or is received from without, process that energy and consciously change it. The same way you resurrect and uplift your own energy field, you can do for others or the collective.

Transform the energy into love through acceptance and conscious alchemy. Accept the energy into your heart and deal with it in your own personal space. It might not be your energy. But you are the bigger person. You are the one with skills to transmute energy. Accept the energy. Be with it. Pretend it is speaking to you and you are listening with compassion. Allow its expression. Then release it. The love in your heart that has accepted it automatically has given it the attention it needs and it has received the higher vibration of your inner light that you have mastered.

Acceptance of others comes from the understanding that everyone is doing the best they can, according to their own understanding of life. In essence we are souls in the process of evolution. Look at people as souls and remember we are developing different aspects of ourselves at different rates. Sometimes when you consciously process energy from others, you are doing a soul service.

In our process of life, we may be at different levels of evolution. This is a fundamental understanding for the awakening soul. From the highest level of perspective, everything and everyone is perfect. That's because the process itself is perfect. We are all heading toward perfection in our own time and manner.

We all have free will and we each are experiencing the effects of our own choices. We cannot choose for others nor can we change them. It is most beneficial just to accept each individual just the way they are. We *can* alter our own choices, however, such as when we are in someone's space who is not treating us well, by removing ourselves from their space. We can accept them and love them from a distance while transforming the energy in our own space back into love. As previously stated, any negative energy they direct at us can also be transformed back into love and sent back to them.

Another method of transforming energy is "**Transmute, Transcend, and Transform.**" Take an emotion such as anger or hurt feelings, for example. The first step is to transmute the energy by being with it rather than trying to bury it or kill it with substances. By sitting and looking straight at the energy, you come to understand it fully and it dissipates.

The second step is to transcend the energy. Rise above the details of the problem and look at the big picture. Look from all angles and perspectives and get all around it. A purpose, awareness, or even a blessing will become evident and you will reach understanding. Being above, rather than a part of this energy creates an observer perspective.

The third step is to transform the energy. Love it for its purpose. Love it for its wisdom. Love the clarity around the message that has surfaced. Thank the energy for its information and its purpose that has been fulfilled, and give it a new purpose with vision—direct it to a new form. As you love the energy, you regain your inner peace. You have changed yourself and you have helped change the world. You feel better and you act out of wisdom with kindness.

Transmute with Vision and Vibration

The highest vibration comes from a pure heart. Our personal and collective evolution is developed by raising the frequency of our heart's radiation by keeping our thoughts centered on Divine Love and service to others, following inspiration, and setting clear divinely inspired intentions. Our center of intelligence comes from our heart. Our mind is attuned to Divine intelligence through our heart by way of the Christ light within.

With resonance to the God-vibration we feel compassion for our fellow man and all life. I sense this vibration of compassion as a violet light, a frequency of pure love that lifts the vibration of all energy with a loving embrace. We are gifted with the violet flame of compassion in our purified hearts, and it holds great power. We can envision this dazzling violet flame embracing and enfolding people or conditions with the intention of lifting the vibrational frequency to release lower conditions that are not of God's perfection. With love and vision, we can use the power of the spoken word to release these higher vibrations out into the world.

Transcending is Uplifting

When energy is transmuted with love, vibrational frequency is enhanced and raised to higher levels. Higher perceptions become possible. The designs of the Immaculate Concept of God's Divine Plan can be apprehended and applied. We establish a higher state of consciousness because we have transcended the lower vibrations. We create a new field of free energy. All energy contains information and is set for a purpose. Once that purpose is completed or transcended through transmutation, it is energy that is free to use for a new purpose. This purpose is infused into the energy through a clear vision of a new perfect outcome. The next step is to give the energy a new purpose.

Transformation of Energy

Energy is transformed, or changed from one form to another, by giving it direction, or purpose. We tune in to our Divinity and feel inspired to direct this energy according to God's will, or what we feel is right in our own soul's wisdom. We are conscious creators centered in peace and goodwill toward all. We are free to create great and wonderful things! Since we are divinely attuned and guided, we sense within the best thing to do with energy in each moment. Our own spirit is uplifted as we create. An effervescent joy bubbles through our spirit.

Lightworkers do this all the time. That's why we are here at this time.

Unity of Purpose

We are all part of the same energetic life system. Your energy is my energy and vice versa. I really appreciate all of your efforts because I know it affects me. I'm doing the same thing for you.

The key is to share this information with many people. Tell them how to create peace on earth. Teach them the process. Have everyone who learns it teach it to as many people as they can, too.

> *It is important at this time to emphasize*
> *personal empowerment*
> *and help people to understand and realize*
> *their full creative powers as individuals.*

These processes will become part of the morphogenic field and many people will discover them on their own. (It really has already been happening since September 11, 2001.)

Surely we will sense a sudden shift in the world and suddenly there will be no negative energy left for people to use unconsciously for hate, greed, or war. There may be a final drama that ushers in this shift. All relationships will have been healed. We will sense the peace on the whole planet and feel a huge relief.

What Needs to be Said

The mark of the person who has not overcome the lower self is that the person would be trying to control the outer world of form, rather than the inner world of vibration.

The more narcissistic, egotistical, and selfish the person is, the more they try to use force upon others to change or control them. Sometimes, they attempt to skirt Universal Law and deceive them out of their free will choice. They may try to use manipulation, deception, or mind control to get the person to do their bidding.

Well, what happens when one attempts to supersede Universal Law? This will become evident as things unfold. Nature has a built-in boomerang. I'll call it a boomerang for balance. The boomerang will present opportunities for one to be humbled and then they will realize that they are subject to Universal Law.

Law is balance.

Narcissism, Egotism, and Selfishness which appears as the shell of the lower self will be transmuted, transcended, and dissolved into the Essence of Being.

Separation is transcended. That's when repentance occurs. Eventually one feels the pain they have caused another. They take responsibility. They turn around. They face their own shadows. They vow to do better. It's a big shift. It's definitely a change of direction—away from fear and hate and towards love and peace.

Those who attune their inner nature to the Cosmic Light live in harmony with God—All That Is—Infinite Intelligence. The amalgamation of soul and spirit is achieved through communion. Meditation and prayer directs the attention inward. This is an operation of Humility.

The lower self is subject to the Higher Self. The Higher Self is a unique expression of the Whole of Self, whole Spirit. It's the mind that creates separation. It's the heart that dissolves it.

The mind, or the ego, does not disappear. It takes its rightful place. It is stellar in its abilities. But it is not the director. It is a tool of consciousness.

God, the Father or Source --- All That Is – is Cosmic Energy in motion and expression. That is Life. Purity of Being is expression of God's love, creativity, healing, enlightenment, joy of giving, and uplifting. There is an attunement to perfection by image transference during vibrational resonance.

Realizing that the True Self is of God, and is God, places the consciousness in its full power. True Self-realization is to be identified as Self. (The self as Whole as opposed to a being separate part.) Since the vibrational attunement is love, peace, and harmony, that is what is created. The myriad expressions of love are divine beauty. If you can sense it, you are in bliss.

Attunement is achieved through surrender, praise, gratitude, and love. Attention to the inner core, or heaven within, emancipates the potential and activates the patterns of perfection. The sublime feelings that come from resonating with the deep peace within create the canvas for perception. Perception becomes inspiration. Inspiration becomes action. Action creates matter—it takes the substance of love, combines it with the images of the mind (imagination), and manifests the vision through attraction and action. It's symbiotic. That's why synchronicities increase.

> *Intelligence is everywhere present.*
> *"In God I live and move and have my Being."*

The very breath of life is creative. It is life flowing. People who learn to live in the flow know grace. They know divine timing. It is peaceful in the flow. What's the rush? We live in Eternity.

Diving into the heaven of your heart reveals a deep heart feeling. It is sensed as complete fulfillment. One realizes that outer circumstances are not the genesis of happiness and love. The generator of the heart leads one into the kingdom of the Soul. In the kingdom of the Soul, the intelligence of the Soul, or part, is merged with Spirit, or the Whole. This is Bliss!

Hanging out in the center of causal creation, or inner direction of attention, or in prayer and meditation, changes the sense of self. It awakens awareness.

Perception becomes advanced. Nobody can really teach this, it has to be experienced through one's own personal journey of discovery. Nobody can activate your potential, but you. Others may inspire you. You may notice through others that it can be done. But you have to activate your own potential. And this is good. This is what brings great joy to your life.

The inner approach to life brings Harmony. Deeper and deeper one goes as we progress. There is no end. It just keeps getting better. The Being just keeps getting better. Old patterns of being give way to new patterns of being.

Vibrations of the heart are purified. Images of the mind are perfected. Once out of victim consciousness, thoughts are pure and creative. No longer dwelling on "what might be," one "lives" in the desired creation.

Now the consciousness has been transformed by overcoming the lower self. Instead of trying to control others, one recognizes the power in controlling one's self—the inner world of thought and feeling. This is the mastery of life energy through vibrational attunement.

This is what the souls of humanity, God's children, are up to. It's the process of Evolution at its finest.

Everything has Purpose. Purpose reveals perfection. Perfection reveals peace.

The Changing of the Guard

We can be thankful for our challenges and problems. As we give gratitude for the impurities of humanity arising in our awareness, we are changing darkness to light. We are Spiritual Warriors! The Light is here. We are in it. We ARE it! As we discover dark deeds and deception, we are changing the guard in terms of leadership on our planet.

The deep state, or cabal, or whatever term you want to use, is being exposed. Anything that is out of God's Divine Order of love is being brought to the light of awareness for healing now because we have the skills. We are prepared and qualified to make the world a better place.

Purified Hearts

The fate of humanity is at hand. We are now in the evolutionary phase of soul advancement because of our purified hearts. We have gone through fires of trials and tribulations individually and collectively. We have witnessed the darkness and our light within keeps shining brighter.

Our divinity is showing up as more love, more compassion, more passion for freedom, and more power to change things. Our souls are activated to discover and express our own unique purpose. That's what passion does. Passion is the fire within. That fire burns off the dross. It erases apathy, illusion, and false programming or belief systems. The fire of passion brings out the best in us. Souls emerge as heroes or heroines and leaders.

We are united so much more as our hearts are purified. We forgive and let go of our mistakes and grievances. We are letting go of things that can be forgiven because, quite frankly, we truly did not know any better. We did not know what we did not know.

As we awaken, each in our own way and each in our own time, we create the space of unconditional love for others to wake up. We rise in our vibration when we seek to understand and to help rather than to judge. It's normal to think, "Why are they so dumb? Why can't they see? Why don't they just wake up?" But therein is our own soul's evolution. We have to be patient. We have to give everyone as much time as they need.

One thing that gives me a sense of compassion is knowing what people have to go through sometimes. There is always impetus to grow or wake up. Each time we don't get the hint of the truth or the lesson, the message keeps getting stronger and louder, and usually more painful. Yikes! To think what some people are going through to wake up. Serious issues. Health, welfare, anxiety from disease, death, loss of income, loss of freedom, assaults by those who abuse their power, and worst of the worst, seeing children suffer.

When you think you've seen it all, along comes another blow. And yet, we get more fire, more passion to change things. We are empowered by our passion. When we are connected to and guided by Source, or God the Father, we use our passionate energy rightly. Our powerful righteousness is changing the landscape of our world.

The fire of passion is purifying our hearts. We are feeling and acting out of our love for all.

Purity Brings Peace

In the depths of our being is the peaceful presence of God. We are one with that vibration. We can remain peaceful while being full of passion. Peace and power is a mighty combination. Centered in God, the light of our souls shines while maintaining the inner peace. While outside we may express the fire of the truth that we know, inside we are at peace and know we are standing for what is right.

Truth is light. Light is might. Do what's right. Stand and fight!

That's how we are uniting to bring peace to our world. We are united by the truth. We are united in the resonate vibration of our pure hearts.

I pray that all receive the peace that passeth all understanding. I pray that all receive peace, perfect health, prosperity, and abundance in our unified field of love consciousness.

Chapter Eleven

THE TRINITY PATTERN
INTEGRATION, ALIGNMENT, AND BALANCE

The Holy Trinity

The most common language when describing and addressing the Holy Trinity is: Father, Son, and Holy Spirit. However, when speaking about these three attributes of God, there are many different forms of expression. God, the Father is also known as Almighty God. He (not referring to male, but to the head of the Holy Trinity which is interwoven into all of Creation) is also referred to as Great Spirit. The Christ Light within also refers to the "still small voice." The still small voice of the Christ Light is our conscience. The Holy Spirit is also known as The Holy Breath, or the Spirit of Truth.

God, the Father is the Most High. Jesus attributes all of His works to God, the Father. "I of myself can do nothing. It is my Father in Heaven who doeth the works." God, the Father is omniscient, omnipotent, and omnipresent. That is, He is all-knowing, all-powerful, and everywhere present. Where does all knowledge come from? Where does all power come from? Where does all awareness come from? Jesus acknowledges that all comes from Father God. Father God is in Heaven. Heaven is within. It's the totality of the One Divine Mind, Cosmic Consciousness, or the Whole Spirit of All. We all have direct access to Father God and His "image" which is all knowledge, all power, and all awareness of everything everywhere.

Because God, our Father is the Source of all, we give Glory to God for all that we are, all that we receive, all that we create, and all that we give. In Him we live and move and have our being. All energy is God. Our Father God is the source of all energy, information, inspiration, desires, provisions, and protection. Everything.

The Christ Light within is our own direct contact with God's Holy presence. It is the reflection of God's light. In order to see a reflection clearly, we get still. Just like when a lake is still and calm, we see the reflection with clarity. During these still moments we reflect the vision and vibration of God, the Father. We get in tune so that we can hear that "still small voice." We commune with God through our Christ Light. That's why Jesus said, no one can get to the Father, except by me. We need to realize that our inner light is the Christ Consciousness that is developed by tuning in to God and listening to our conscience, that "still small voice." It brings the soul so much peace to sit in the vibration of God's presence through communion, prayer, meditation, and contemplation. Through our Christ Light, we reach the zero point center of consciousness and perceive the clear image of God, of God's plans, and our own unique pattern. We are guided according to our personal blueprint, our own design written in the seed of our soul. We feel a sense of inner approval when we do good, or make the highest choice. When we listen to the intrinsic wisdom within, we no longer seek outer approval or flattery for a sense of self-worth. Self-worth comes from within.

Not only is the Christ Light the doorway to God, the Father, but this Christ Light that Jesus demonstrated as the perfect pattern for humanity, is also the bringer of the Holy Spirit of Truth. For by following the Christ Light, each soul increases their vibrational frequency and attunes to the God vibration that resonates, and brings awareness of Truth to the conscious mind. The Spirit of Truth grows stronger. We increase our strength of character. We truly feel this inner strength and the power we have. We know we are sovereign and stand for freedom. We deepen and expand our consciousness and perceptions. We raise our consciousness and evolve to higher states of being. The evidence of increasing abilities of this human evolution is the increase in discernment. We can distinguish between what is true, and what is not true. The more we develop, then less chance we have of being deceived.

The relationship of God, the Father, the Christ Light within expressing as conscience, and the Holy Spirit of Truth is paradoxically sequential and also intertwined. The key is looking within and finding and following the intelligence of the Christ Light. You don't have to be Christian to know that the Christ Light is found within every Child of God. Some people might follow Christian principles and not even know it as such! Maybe some have confused Christianity with man-made dogma, tradition, rules, or beliefs that are not of God. Certainly there are traps to follow a "leader" or "priest" or "expert" that supposedly know the only true and right answer or decision to make that lead one into a ditch of destruction. But the direct contact with God, the Father our true Source of life, and light, and love, and liberty, is direct inner contact. It does not matter that we may have different names for the higher intelligence. The truth is that everyone has access to it. I think that's what humanity is learning at this time: "Go Direct!" and don't be deceived.

When we are tuned in to this higher power and highest intelligence, our intuition provides us with the information we seek. We get the message that guides us to make a right choice, or to avoid a pitfall. There are a variety of communication tools that different people use. We are not the same and we don't always speak the same language about it, but we all have direct connection.

We Perpetually Receive Love from God

First of all, we are constantly receiving gifts from our Almighty Father God. We receive His Spirit—the pure goodness of Spirit. Always refreshing and renewing and perfecting, His Spirit is the very breath of Life. We are truly blessed. This breath of life alchemizes our soul. As we face this spiritual light with our attention within, we come to know our true eternal self and the essence of Truth that we are, a truth born of Love, and a pure Love born of God.

Our gifts come to us on every plane of existence. We receive love and lessons of love. We are blessed with all that meets our physical needs. We are blessed with spiritual gifts of love, peace, and many good feelings. Our gifts include ideas, inspiration, and creative solutions. We are attuned to get wise divine guidance.

We are led to know truth. We are delivered from misguided programs and agendas that are not for our highest good. In knowing the truth we unite with our brothers and sisters who are also following God's ways of goodness. Jesus was our perfect pattern. "Follow me" were his words. Jesus brought many gifts to humanity and showed us how to stay attuned to God. He teaches by example as he shows us what our potentials are.

In the process of becoming our best and highest actualized potential, we receive the Spirit of God. We become more and more like Him until He becomes us and we realize our true spiritual nature. We absorb His Spirit. This is what we integrate.

We become purified, perfected, and purposeful masters of energy, of information, of the substance of life: Love. We learn to generate and amplify the love. We emanate and radiate the light of love. We are molding the ethers of love to form gases, and liquids, and solids as we alchemically form and change the substance of spirit, the substance of us, which we all know by now is love.

The Patterns of Trinity

The patterns of trinity are expressed in many ways: Father, Mother, Child; Father, Son, Holy Spirit; Left brain, Right brain, Heart; Creator, Creating, Created; Proton, Neutron, Electron; and so on.

The basis of the patterns of trinity is God, the One Spirit—Father. The dual nature of God-Spirit is Infinite Intelligence (Christ Light) and Force (The power of the Holy Spirit of Truth). Married, they bear the child of Love. That's perfect balance. The deepest perception of heart intelligence is the knowing of the Absolute, the Eternal, that which never changes. Force comes from will. It is the all-powerful essence of Divine Purpose that all harmony is based on. Harmony with Divine Will is aligning with the power of God. When the inner knowing of Absolute Truth is wedded to the power of Divine Will (harmonious purpose), creative cooperation bears the child of love. It is a heart glue!!! It feels great! Universal Love is divine. The pure love born of God resides in every heart. It is Christ.

Christ arise!!! Realization brings activation and actualization of the soul's inherent qualities. Each Christed, or activated soul, senses their Divine purpose. They know their mission. They perceive their soul's blueprint. The soul's blueprint is an exact puzzle piece that is part of the Divine Plan.

The Divine Plan is based on the Holy Trinity. It is God's perfect expression of love within each person. When we know we are a Child of God, we know we are here to express God's love. It's as simple as that.

Consciousness is Evolving

The more we blend with the Spirit of God, the more we receive and integrate spirit, the higher we advance in the spectrum of evolution. We are humble beings. We know we need God and that God is our Source. Our direct connection to Source leads us to inevitable good.

We are completing the era of preparation. We are entering the era of application. Here's where the rubber meets the road. All of our challenges in the world at this time are giving us the catalyst for our soul's evolution. We are receiving opportunities to put our prepared and qualified souls to the test. As we are tested, we are refining our consciousness. We are fine tuning our consciousness as we turn to the light of the soul that is amalgamated to God-Spirit. We are engaging in an expression of empowerment every time we stand up for truth and freedom. Each time we stand in unity, against the forces of evil that wish to divide us, we are increasingly activating our soul qualities and potential. We are becoming empowered, and really feeling our power. We are really feeling our power of unity.

The collective consciousness is evolving as we individually evolve and unite in the vibration of the spirit of love. The spirit of love is coming from inside of us. It is the essence of our Christed soul in expression. We are creating huge powerful fields of energy. We keep feeling this power more and more every day. It is breaking down the old power structure.

The power of love is dismantling the programmed belief systems that could exist when we were in fear or victim consciousness. The sheer number of people waking up is accelerating. We are reaching critical mass in terms of a united spirit of awakened souls. By the time many people read this, we will have surpassed this critical mass. We will be building our new world as Heaven on Earth, each according to our own soul's purpose. We have been purified, perfected, and have aligned with Divine Purpose and harmoniously cooperate as we achieve our soul's mission and perfect actualized expression of our highest potential.

Those of us who embody the new race consciousness are the builders. There are varying phases that exist simultaneously. There is an overlap during the transition of the old and the new. However, the old is fast dissolving. The new is already taking shape.

The Holy Trinity continues to give birth to Love.

Three Keys in the Transformation of Consciousness

Consciousness is Light. We are generating, receiving, and integrating a *new* light. The new light is a field of consciousness that is an upgrade from our former selves and way of being.

Integration has to do with fully receiving and accepting and embodying the light that catalyzes the higher states of consciousness. We are activated. We notice perception changes as the new light assimilates within our energy field. Our ability to discern is increased. Our intuition is stronger.

Alignment is getting all of our aspects of being on the same page. We put our mind and intellect, our physical body and our personal energy, our feelings and emotions into alignment with our soul-intentions.

These four major aspects of Self need to be kept in balance: mind, body, heart, and soul. We stay centered in peace when we practice balanced development.

According to Jesus, the Universal God is wisdom, will, and love. He says that all people worship the One God, but not all see him alike. They see a part of God and take it for the all. (*Aquarian Gospel of Jesus the Christ*, by Levi) People have different names for God, and different ideas of what God is. From this stem their ideals and what standards, principles, and values they choose to live by.

The triune nature of God is all encompassing as the Father, Son, and Holy Spirit. The attributes of God are omniscience, omnipresence, and omnipotence. God is All-Knowing, Everywhere-Present, and All-Powerful. God is the creator, creating, and created, all in one. The knower, the knowingness, and the known is God. Awareness of all; subjective and objective, all at once. And like the atom: neutron, proton, and electron; or neutral, positive, and negative. All in balance.

In God's wisdom, there is purpose, a grand design unfolding. In God's will, there is power. And in God's love there is the Light of Truth, or Holy Spirit, everywhere present.

Integration

We are all receiving an influx of light on planet Earth. The Schumann resonance, the frequency of the Earth has typically run at about 7.83 hertz. However, continual measurement of the Schumann resonance demonstrates that we are receiving spikes in energy as the sun emits high frequency Mass Corona Emanations. Our body, mind, and spirit responds. We feel the need to ground the energy by walking barefoot on the ground, or sometimes we just need to rest or sleep as we ground and integrate the high frequency light energy.

It is my perception that our DNA is being activated. My intuitive knowing has always been that we would recover our lost powers and abilities. For example, our ability to naturally pick up on energy fields of information increases our telepathic communication. Light is consciousness; information and the knowing of vast ideas, solutions, inventions, and creative inspiration. It's our essential makeup as spirit BE-ings.

We consciously receive God's light also from within which is our Source of wisdom. We are open to receive the light of Christ Consciousness, God Consciousness, and Cosmic Consciousness. This is the essence of our True Self. We know when we go there that we are eternal essence of awareness. Wisdom pours through our soul and into our hearts as we commune with God. As we receive and contemplate this inner light of wisdom, and then live it, we ascend to higher and higher states of consciousness. We integrate the Spirit of God into our lives.

But now, it's new. We're being upgraded. We've been preparing for this and we are ready. Our conscious evolution of raising our vibration has equipped us to receive this new upgraded light that is increasing our latent perceptive abilities.

As we integrate this new light, it's like weaving ourselves into God, and allowing God to weave new levels of wisdom into our very being at all levels. Our interdimensional nature is becoming apparent.

We get epiphanies, or "Ah-Ha!" moments. The truth is realized! It hits home. We know it, and we know we know it. We live it and become it. We embody truth. This is all part of integration.

"Let there be light!" Let us realize the light that we are, and that we keep getting more.

Alignment

When we choose to consciously align with God's will and God's Divine Plan, our desires transform. We come into accordance with our own soul's blueprint. We discover our own design and purpose. Our talents and gifts become more evident. We get a rudder on our ship of life and we have clear direction.

"Christ Light stand forth and take command!" "God's Will be done!" We can use such directives to put order into our consciousness. We align with the power of God. We become powerful as we do this. This is felt in the body as power. The power of the Inner Light IS in control, consciously. Our intelligence increases; it takes a step up.

Our perceptions are deeper and clearer. Fear dissolves. Our thought patterns transform. Our identity shifts. Our heart expands.

We learn to live a Spirit-guided life.

As we embrace our power and our sovereignty, we realize we are in control of ourselves. Our eternal essence is spirit and our soul is individualized spirit that makes each one of us unique. As spirit we have the qualities of God when we are attuned to Divine Mind. We may be anywhere or everywhere present, or we may express our Divine power through will, intentions, and thoughts. When we surrender our will (and sense of separate self) and replace that with attunement to Divine will we are one with the infinite intelligence of the universe. We experience harmony.

Each of our other aspects, Mind, Heart-emotions, and Body should be subjected to the soul for optimum functionality.

We can make inner statements according to our Divine will that puts all of our aspects into alignment. We can say: "My heart is pure and is subject to my soul, my mind is subject to my heart, and my body is subject to my mind." All is one in spirit: united with the highest vibration of love. Thoughts are controlled from within. Attention is given to the inner life as a priority.

Developing Listening Grace through meditation and prayer, one travels up the levels of vibration and begins to create a new baseline of consciousness. For example, when we meditate on a regular basis, we delve into the well of peace within God's presence. We hang on to that peace longer and longer after we meditate. Eventually, our countenance and demeanor become stabilized in a peaceful vibration. Things don't bother us as much. We become more neutral in our observations of outer life.

There's a lot more to that type of energy mastery when you are empathic. Other vibrational frequencies are picked up and felt as within our own field. But we do learn to transmute that energy. We also learn to draw boundaries and discard old ways of being that include drama. We don't need drama any longer. Drama was just an old way to get someone's energy when we didn't know how to get it straight from our Source within.

Our heart does receive. We don't have to accept or buy into other people's drama, or ploys to usurp our energy. Manipulators are adept at stealing other people's energy. One way manipulators steal energy is through our emotions. As empathic beings, we first get battered around emotionally until we figure out what's going on. We can be controlled through our emotions.

One time, I was onto the tricks of an energy vampire. I observed how she made my friend feel guilty by a statement that she made. Next, she asked him to do something. He agreed immediately because she was in control of his emotions. Once I pointed out how the manipulation was occurring, he saw it, too, and put a stop to it.

Manipulation through emotions is a "back door" into our consciousness. This "back door" circumvents our own decision-making by undermining our conscience and common sense. We inadvertently give up control of our mind. This can be accomplished from person to person, or from mass media to mass population, or through inculcation in education, and also through a subtle process of disintegrating morals and ethics by mental conditioning and rationalization.

People who develop a strong conscience through a direct connection with God are not so easily tricked, deceived, or abused. That's one reason why it is critically important to do inner work. Inner work is really not work in the traditional sense. It's actually the opposite. It's just taking time to get still and be. It could be just being in nature. It could be meditation and communion with God. It could be honest self-reflection. Our True Self is naturally all-knowing, wise, peaceful, loving, compassionate, and forgiving.

One serious way people have been tricked is that they are lead to believe that their identity is totally physical. The right brain and imagination which are doors to our Higher Self, our soul, are discredited. The left brain and hard evidence of physical data are adhered to as a limited sense of self. Some people think they are just the body, just a mortal physical body, and that pleasing the carnal desires of the flesh is what life is all about. That is a disconnected life—a life without spiritual understanding.

When our identity is founded in spirit, we have that connection that gives us a sense of wholeness. Connection feels like love. It's not something you can measure, but you sure know what love feels like.

When we truly know what love feels like, and we identify with that, we grow out of patterns of fear, guilt, and anger. We don't deny or suppress our feelings. Oh no—just the opposite. We love our feelings and transmute them into information. Then we make conscious choices.

Also, when we keep our vibrations high, we cannot be controlled by those lower vibrational feelings. Step by step, we realize our power to master feelings through vibration. And the more we do, the more we only resonate with truth. We just don't buy into any ridiculous lies like we once did out of sheer lack of understanding of our own ability to master vibration.

Our heart is a radio frequency transmitter that controls the ethers through our thoughts and intentions. Peace and love and gratitude is the focus for high vibrational mastery. It's a journey. It's is a journey that we are taking together.

Listening Grace, Harmony, Letting Go, and Going with the Flow

Communion with God develops union with God, and with union comes listening grace. Listening grace is a constant tuning in to the voice of God within. Like a constant companion and guiding light, it is a comfort in all storms and a rock to stand on.

Harmony is another gift of spirit that lends peace to the mind and heart. If peace is attacked, then the well of the soul can once again be entered to regain harmony and equilibrium. There is a center and everything else just flows around it. That's that rock—always there.

If thoughts or impressions from experiences disturb us mentally or emotionally, again we go back to the rock. We just let go. We describe what is troubling us, and then lift it up to God to take care of. All concerns are diminished, all heaviness lifted, all problems relieved when we talk to God and hand over what may cause us distress, anxiety, or trouble.

Once we let go, we are free to go with the flow. The flow of life is simple and natural. We just do the next right thing. If we are unsure, all we have to do is ask. Asking is the best way to move forward. It activates spirit. Ask and flow. It's such a happy and peaceful journey!

Balance

We have four main aspects of our life: physical, mental, emotional, and spiritual. They are all interrelated in our wholeness of being. When we develop one aspect, it has an effect on all the other aspects. We need to constantly come into balance and keep our center. Our center of inner focus establishes and maintains the peace within our being, the peace within our lives, and the peace within our world.

We are constantly bombarded by energies which by virtue of their vibrational frequencies that can alter our sense of peace, or the higher vibrational frequency to which we have attained in our quiet, still moments of prayer and meditation. These present a dissonance, or contrast. In this period of human evolution, we are learning to transmute these energies. We are being given tools and processes of consciousness to raise the energies rather than let them lower ours and disturb our peace. What a gift these challenges bring!

Through our challenges, our gifts of higher consciousness are being activated. They say necessity is the mother of invention, and it's the essence of this notion that applies.

Hold your peace. Keep your center. Feel your inner strength increase.

Balanced Development

One way to maintain equilibrium is through balanced development. While we are consciously evolving, we are reaching toward greater and greater accomplishments by setting personal goals. When we set goals for ourselves, we can do this in a holistic manner. We take into account each aspect of our being and what we wish to develop in that area. In one of my programs, I provide an activity where you write down your goals while considering each aspect of being.

We always start right where we are at. So, first we do an assessment of each area: Physical—Health, Mental—Creative expression and material needs, Emotional—relationships and prioritizing response of love over reactionary expressions, and Spiritual—developing strong connections to the Eternal Oneness, or growing ever closer to God, and developing deep spiritual perceptions that feed our souls. To assess each area we contemplate the state of being in each aspect of our lives and determine whether we are in the "Repair" or "Maintenance" or "Development" stage. For example, if we are going through a divorce we assess the area of relationships as a "Repair" stage, and we set goals accordingly. If we are going to school to earn a degree, learning a skill, or building a business based on our creative talents, then we are in the "Development" state in the mental category. An example of the "Maintenance" level would be if we are at a stable equilibrium and things are going along fine as they are such as when we are working harmoniously within our home with our family. That would be considered the stage for our emotional, or relationship, category.

If we put too much time into our work and ignore our home and family, we may get out of balance. Or, if we work too much and ignore our health needs for play and rest, we may get out of balance. By spreading our attention, time, and efforts consciously to each area of our lives, we can maintain a sense of balance and avoid self-made disasters born of inharmonious living.

Staying in balance requires a conscious lifestyle.

The Powers of the Soul

Within us is the wisdom of God. Enjoy the direct connection to God as a baby in the womb derives its nourishment from the umbilical cord which connects it to its mother. It is natural. We know this connection when we go within. It is so important to realize and utilize this direct connection.

We are connected by breath and communication. Sound and light travel through air and water. Sometimes, when we feel love the deepest, we cry. The water flows through our hearts and spills out into our eyes. This depth of love occurs naturally. We can tap into it consciously and become highly aware at all times.

Quick moments of stillness and checking in within keep this connection and the powers of our soul-Spirit in our awareness.

Our true identity is of the Whole Self; the Real Self of our Whole Being in the seed of our soul. Going into the heaven within our hearts and souls transforms our being and consciousness. We are processing energy and information differently now.

It can't be stated often enough: "Be still." The powers of the soul are derived from an inner life of prayer and contemplation, in meditation and communion. The humbled ego-mind gives way to the higher intelligence of the soul which knows its home in Spirit. Go home into your heart. Breathe and relax. It's not all about doing and getting any longer.

It's all about identifying with the light of God as the source of all intelligence. Once connected firmly, conscience grows, evolves, and guides to higher and higher vibrational frequencies.

We are going to be amazed at what unfolds over the next few years!

Mastering Consciousness

We are becoming masters of consciousness. We are doing that by delving deep into the roots of our True Self. Our True Self-awareness is a product of soul-searching, self-reflection, humble asking within, perceiving the realm of the Absolute Eternal God-Spirit, praying to God, meditating on spiritual truth, contemplating in a state of curiosity, opening our minds and hearts to receive the higher vibrations, attuning to Divine will, surrendering selfish self to attune to Divine Oneness of Whole Universal Self, opening our hearts and minds to new ideas and inspiration and intuition. Deep perception makes many masters.

Every step we take to exit the mayhem of the outer world to explore inner space renders a great benefit to the soul. We have so many ways to do this. Each individual uses many avenues, and some prefer certain soul experiences over others, but we all "get there" and it doesn't matter how.

Some enter the realm of the spirit life through being in nature and listening to the birds, loving the trees, watching the water, feeling the breeze, adoring the beauty, and feeling the essence. Sometimes we just find quiet solitude and go within while voicing our concerns to relieve our earthly burdens and request assistance. Or sometimes we read inspirational literature and feel the resonance of meaning for our life at the present time. At times we are in the zone of inspired creativity and we flow with the passion of ideas flowing while sensing the joy of expression. Whatever the method, the feeling is terrific!!!

We really ARE conscious creators. We really ARE mastering consciousness. We really ARE truly blessed!

Chapter Twelve

A PERSONAL PATH TO LIGHT

Transformation of Consciousness

Transformation is upliftment of vibration. Transformation is expansiveness in both scope and depth of perception, awareness, and beingness. Transformation moves the sense of self from the personal to the universal. Identity shifts.

In our material world, we are programmed to think of ourselves as physical. But once we have contact with our internal spirit, and maintain that connection through constant communion, our identity shifts to our universal self. We acquire the sense of our Eternal essence, our True Self.

We are pure love at our core. We are Absolute Truth at our core. We are the sum of all truth and of all love. We are at zero point consciousness where all is whole, all is in harmony and balance, and all is known directly and instantly. We know we are creating according to the immaculate concept of God, the One Great Intelligent Cosmic Mind.

The transformation of consciousness is the root of personal and global evolution. We naturally progress lifeward as we overcome difficulties, challenges, trials, and tribulations.

It seems like if we don't take the natural approach to transformation, the universe will provide more challenges to the point of cataclysm to help us wake up and realize our True Selves and our True Power.

Think of all you have gone through the last few years. Reflect on all the changes in your life. Consider how much you have changed because of all of it. Life is different now. You are different. We are all changing. We are becoming masters through the challenges that life has dealt us. I don't know anyone who hasn't felt this unprecedented change. We are at a precipice. It seems our freedom is at stake. It seems humanity is at stake.

We are sovereign beings. We maintain our freedom, unless we relinquish it. We are free in our minds; unless we give up that freedom of thought and allow other outer influences to take over. We can govern ourselves. We don't need to consent to any imposition upon our freedom. Freedom starts from within.

It is imperative at this time to claim and maintain our freedom and know our true power. The stakes are high and we must consider future generations.

This is why the transformation of consciousness is so vitally critical at this time in human history.

We need everyone to wake up and express their highest potential. Everyone has a part; a purpose. We need you.

There is assistance available to help. There is guidance from within and all around. We are creating a field of love. We are all family. All the ones who are awakened are helping others to awaken, just like a big brother or sister would help their younger siblings.

All of humanity is awakening. Our galactic family is here to greet us. We are ready.

With all veils of separation dissolving, we are set to experience reunions. Great things are on the horizon for each of us; for all of humanity!

An Individual Experience of the Universal Transformation of Consciousness

While there is a universality of the evolution of humanity's collective consciousness, we each have our own unique experiences of the inherent fundamental life changes that the shift consists of. It is symbiotic. We are affecting the collective consciousness and we are affected by our surrounding vibrational frequencies of the overall field of consciousness.

The extent to which we are affected, and the degree to which we effect the collective consciousness depends on our level of development and how much we have gained equilibrium and authority over our own energy field. We will eventually reach the paradoxical position of being one with the whole Spirit and at the same time being singular and sovereign.

The Personal Path of Transformation

The renovation of consciousness includes inner revelations and realizations that change our sense of identity, how we process information and experiences, our assessment of our moral and ethical standards and how we live up to them, the principles of life that we idealize and strive to live up to, what we value, our desires and goals—and then there is an additional factor that becomes prevalent: the meaning and purpose for our lives. We become impelled and inspired to contribute to and serve Life and humanity according to our innermost passion.

Who Do You Think You Are? The Identity Shift

The general influences that formed our self-concept were framed in a materialistic paradigm. We started being evaluated by what we looked like, what we had, or the status that we gained from our employment. So many times, people would ask as a primary question: "What do you do for a living?" Of course the answer to this question would convey the information to make an assessment based on material values. So, if you were a doctor or lawyer, or executive in a large corporation, or had governmental powers of some sort, you would be thought of in a higher light in terms of your net worth. On the other hand, if your position was of a general laborer, or stay at home mother, clerk of some kind, then your perceived worth would be lower in stature.

We built an "ego" or "alter" sense of self from this value system. We bought into it for a while. Our appearance in terms of size, shape, and clothing had an effect on our perceived sense of self and self-worth. Our car model, our job title, our home, our level of education—all of these things combined to give us a sense of pseudo-self.

Now, during the transformation of consciousness, we are developing a new sense of self—a greater sense of self. We are discovering our inherent personal value. We realize we have Great Self-Worth!!! It's a process. It requires the inner work of True Self-discovery. But, it feels great! It is the Truth of who we really are.

We are souls. We are children of God. We have a purpose. God knows and loves each one of us. We are each unique and special in our own way. We each are like a special instrument in God's universe, and as we shine, we play the tune of our own soul in such a way that the symphony of life is greater for our presence and participation. We each hold such great value.

When our identity shifts from material and physical, we identify with the essential nature of our soul. We find peace. We realize that wisdom dwells within us. We have full access to the Light of Truth.

When we place our attention in our own hearts and commune with God, the Light Within, we realize more and more the treasures we own in the nature of our true essence—our soul. This is the kingdom of Heaven within.

We are home in our hearts. It's a place for our awareness to go. The inner world awaits discovery by many lost souls. Once found, life will never be the same. It will only get better and better. We have thus found the treasure!

More and more people are realizing that setting aside time daily for introspection, prayer, and meditation increases the quality of life. The moments spent in resting in the peace within has a great impact on our lives and our world. When we commit to coming into balance—the inner and outer life, BE-ing in balance with DO-ing, stillness in balance with movement—we dive daily into the treasures of our own soul. Gifts discovered within are not of this world. They are deeper, more valuable, and eternal. We only open up to them as we become identified as a soul and use our soul's ability to perceive the subtle vibrations that come with a life of inner peace.

And now, with so much at stake in the world it is imperative. It's like we have to make this shift to survive and thrive. We need all of our powers to throw off the old patterns of destruction and corruption and build a better world. So we delve within. We get saturated in inner peace. We know our natural sovereignty as spiritual beings and we feel our power. We demand that peace take hold in our world.

This is what changes, or shifts, our sense of identity. This is the treasure we are all looking for. This is where we receive unlimited vitality and passion and inspiration and enthusiasm for life!

Because so many people are discovering these inner resources, the world is rapidly changing. So much more light is coming into our world. It exposes the darkness of secrets, lies, and evil deeds. These things are coming into our awareness for healing. We have the opportunity to apply love in the form of understanding, compassion, and mercy.

During this time of rapid inner change, we discover that we are Light Warriors activated to make changes! We won't allow the evil to continue. This is part of the changing of the guard discussed in chapter ten.

Our spiritual identity is Light. Light is the Holy Spirit of Truth. The wholeness constitutes the essence of Love. We are purified Light Beings expressing Pure Love.

Our individual identity is realized as a unique soul. All unique souls are part of the whole, like a facet on a diamond. We are treasured.

Processing Experiences, Energy, and Information

Life is made of energy. Everything is energy. Energy contains information. We are aware of ourselves as a set of information called self-concept. Our self-concept is based on what we are aware of. Our Universal mind is a big dynamic database of stored information. We can call it memory. Even scientists relegate the substance of the Universe as "mind stuff".

We are energy beings processing energy information through our mind, or heart, or soul, or a combination of all three. We receive information through outer mediums or directly as pure thought. We receive impressions of information through our feelings.

The center of our awareness has typically been in our head or brain. We think with our rational mind. But now there is a shift: our heart intelligence is activated. Our soul perceptions are being realized. Changes are taking place as far as what or how we process information. Our awareness has expanded.

First of all, we change what we pay attention to. In other words, the input changes. We process the input of information from our experiences and perceptions. We are more sensitive to the information within the energy as a result of our shift in consciousness.

The fact that we consciously "process" is new in our current state of development. In the past, we would just react with raw feelings, or emotionally charged thoughts. Now, we take the time to reflect. We process from a higher perspective and through deeper perception. We look at information in the sense of looking at the bigger picture. We "transcend" the input, or the origination of the experience or information, and become an observer. We become neutral. We can see in and out and all sides. We can *feel into* the energy.

Now, instead of reacting, *we respond*. We can speak objectively and calmly regarding the information that we understand. With the broader perspective, we look for purpose and meaning. We look for lessons. We take responsibility. We apply and increase our understanding.

This leads to more love and peace in our lives and our world.

We feel the energy behind words. We can feel if there is resistance, a disconnect, or anger. We "read" energy. We "speak to" the energy. We use our innate intelligence of empathy to discern what the truth is. We recognize if someone is coming from their ego-mind or from their heart-centered Real Self.

When we process our experiences through inner reflection and contemplation, we elicit more information and gain deeper understanding. We are then able to communicate honestly and openly with the truth that we have discerned.

In fact, our ability to discern is increasing in greater and greater degrees. This processing through soul-perception, or heart intelligence, is changing our relationships. In a group of awakened individuals, the level of communication is through a high vibrational attunement and resonance is felt. Ideas flow more readily because minds and hearts are clear and open.

Assessing our Moral and Ethical Standards

The beautiful thing about what's wrong in our world is that it elicits what is right from the depths of our soul through our conscience and into our conscious awareness. Our conscience is the Light of Truth that we develop as we evolve.

For example, as the trend of "moral relativism" emerges through social engineering, those who are awakening will say: "No! I feel strongly within myself that this is not right." Moral relativism is basically saying that there is no distinct right and wrong, it's all just a matter of perspective.

That sounds like a lukewarm washtub full of hogwash to me. My conscience clearly indicates that some things are definitely wrong, while other things are definitely right. For example, harming an individual, especially a child: Wrong! Conversely, helping someone in need, lending a hand, expressing kindness to someone who needs uplifting: Right!

God unites us in the spirit of love. As we each turn to God individually, we naturally learn the ways of love and express from that understanding. We keep increasing our ability to love as we value truth and purify our intentions. We purify our hearts and we have this inner vision, this inner love intelligence that is our true nature.

What's wrong in our world is that people with selfish intentions and sickened moral standards and ethics through the sublimation of conscience and the elevation of ego and narcissism have sought to become powerful leaders. They have deceived the majority of people through decades and centuries of fear-based activities. They seek to hoard resources, control us, and control the world. They seek to usurp the power of God!

During this period of transformation, we are developing our conscience, illuminating our Inner Light, and discerning what is true and right. Our morals are inherently within us. Our ethical behavior and level of integrity is of high value to us because we know we are building our character that matches our Divine nature.

Chords of Being

We are instruments. Our nature is to harmonize. Our hearts are our tuning forks. Our vibration is pure love.

When we are tuned to the vibration of love, our consciousness strikes the chord of Truth. We are not swayed by "relative" truth. Oh no. It's much deeper than that. Attunement to pure divine love opens the consciousness portal to Absolute Truth—pure direct inner knowing.

Attunement to the Absolute activates the ability of the consciousness to discern. Truth is one. Absolute Truth does not change. It is pure light. Pure light uplifts the soul, our spiritual nature. We see our own reflection—our True Self. Our essential, eternal, True Self is whole, divine, and harmonious. With True Self realized as our true identity, we perceive and express our real nature which is pure love.

As instrumental beings all of our chords lead us to direct inner knowing. We perceive our true identity and all of our abilities of perception are activated and expressed. This True Self-realization and perception activation causes us to know our sovereignty. We are empowered. We are strong light beings of the realm of Absolute Truth.

"Know Thy Self" is the most powerful guidance for the Children of God. Our spirituality is the true essence of our humanity. It is the core of our being. How do we know this essential self that we are? "Be still and know." It's as simple as that.

When we are still, motionless and peaceful, we see the reflection of our own perfection with our inner perception. We tap our deeper intelligence. We see with an inner eye that is in the center of Being. We naturally harmonize with the greater whole; All That Is.

We achieve wholeness of mind.
Our consciousness is expanded.
Awareness is deep.

When we activate the chord of consciousness that leads us to Absolute Truth, we feel satiated. Our soul is in unity with the Source of Light. We "see" that we are pure love and we resonate with that highest vibration.

Life changes.

Peace "that passes all understanding" becomes more and more a part of life until it is constant. Inner peace is achieved.

When we strike the chord of peace, it's like a soul massage. Talk about Heaven!!! Oh, does it ever feel deeply satisfying. Once you feel Heaven, you never want to leave.

One chord plays upon another. The chords of joy and bliss are at hand. The blessings of inner peace, joy, love and happiness play a beautiful heavenly song of Wholeness.

The One rejoices in a harmonious symphony of attuned souls. This kingdom of pure love consciousness is where humanity is heading. No matter what the journey appears to be, this is our next destiny of evolution on the map of Eternity.

Purity, Purpose, and Perfection

Transformation of consciousness involves purifying the heart, discovering one's true purpose in life, and becoming a perfected being according the soul's blueprint—God's immaculate concept of perfect individualized activated and expressed potential.

Everyone is a genius. Everyone has gifts within. Everyone has unique qualities, talents, and passions. The more one purifies the capacity of love within the heart, the more the individual purpose is revealed and perceived within. Infinite ideas and inspiration flow. Vitality of life and the passion for purpose becomes a great motivator.

Purity

Purity happens the more we let go of selfish desires and start doing more and more for others. This is evidence of overcoming the small selfish self and expanding to the universal self where love flows freely.

Intrinsic value is that inner feeling from the soul that indicates the right path. While principle, morals, and ethics are impeccably adhered to, we operate from a place of purity that expands our feeling of love and we just feel so inspired to be kind, to help, and to give. It feels good when we help others—extra good. It's not the same kind of good we feel when we obtain something we want. That kind of feeling is more a flash in the pan. It doesn't last as long. It has no depth like intrinsic value. Our Eternal essential self is providing that feeling of intrinsic value. It is a clue and confirmation that we are expressing our Higher Self and our true nature.

Purpose

Purpose gives meaning to life. It provides us with a reason for being. It is a motivator. When we discover our innermost passion, what stirs us the most, what we care about fervently, it's like we have a rudder for our ship. We know it's time to set sail on a new journey…a journey of expressing our soul's potential.

How do we discover our purpose? We ask. We explore our heart and soul with questions and contemplation. We seek the knowledge that is inherent in our innermost being. We find our soul's blueprint.

As soon as we ask, the fire in our heart stirs. The whole of the universe answers. Synchronicities occur as we are alert to clues that pop up along life's path. And it might not be one big thing all at once. It could be we have bits to give all along the way. Sharing with whoever is around us. Caring for those in our orbit. Just being kind. Then, one things leads to another. As we draw nearer and nearer to our own essential eternal spirit, our soul, we get inspired. Our passion increases. Opportunities arise. We get very clear what IS ours to do, and what is NOT ours to do.

As we assess the state of our communities, nations, and world and feel great dismay at the failing systems we once knew and were a part of, then we step up to the plate to make the world a better place according to the skills and talents that we have developed. We just use them in new and innovative ways in order to overcome the disruption of the old systems.

We make goals and plans. We overcome challenges along the way. We learn to remove ourselves from the old life of drama, distractions, and derailment. We get more and more focused. We overcome or remove obstacles. We evolve all along the way. The journey makes us into masters.

With a pure heart and a clear mind, we learn to be more attuned to spirit and that dissolves the old way of being and all the old programs. We shift our consciousness by using affirmations and paying attention to higher vibrational beings and messages of truth. We see beyond the pitfalls of deception.

With our souls being amalgamated with spirit, we are not deceived or controlled. Fear is a thing of the past. "Perfect love casts out all fear." We just know.

> *"You are an especially designed creation, you have a particular mission, you have a light to give, a work to do that no other can give or accomplish; and if you will open your heart, mind, and soul wide to spirit, you will learn of it in your own heart."*
>
> Jesus
> The Life & Teaching of the Masters of the Far East, Vol. II
> Baird T. Spalding

Perfection

As we become still and reflect the immaculate concept of God's Divine Plan and our part in it, we are sculpted by God's Hand. Our consciousness is alchemized by the light. We ARE the light reflecting perfection.

Even our body becomes light. We transfigure and overcome death.

As we realize our Universal Oneness, we swim in the ocean of love, light, and perfection. We have the perfect vibration of pure love. We hold the vision of perfection that comes from spirit. We ARE light, we ARE pure love, and we stabilize this new perfected consciousness and reflect perfection.

A Life of Service

We are each called to discover our own unique Divine potential. Our joy comes from knowing and expressing the gifts and talents of our own soul. It is an honor and privilege to be a contributor to all of life through service. Every soul has its unique gifts that are needed in our world, especially now.

Once activated through the catalysts of challenges and change, the light of our path becomes more brilliant.

As we take our concerns within, the peace of God that we

experience there, transforms all potential problems into the wisdom that is required to overcome them.

Reflect on Your Perfect Life Experiences

One good way to begin discovering your personal path to light and your personal purpose is to take time to reflect upon all of the experiences you've had. This may take many sessions of contemplation because each one requires a depth of perception, and a higher awareness perspective.

Every experience you have ever had is perfect. It has a good God Purpose. It has made you who you are today. And just in case you need another reminder: *You are perfect just as you are and you are loved exactly for who you are right now.*

God raises us individually and loves us unconditionally. God knows us each by our unique vibrational frequency. God cares deeply. God is inherent and responsive.

One practice that is truly a Divine experience is to just go within and tell God that you want to feel His love. Another is to express to God how much you love Him. Feel love deeply. You can dwell in this state of consciousness for a while and experience extreme peace and love. You may feel strong energy in your heart. You might feel like crying. Your cup may "runneth over" as you fill your heart with the Love of God.

In this place of deep communion, look over your life. Ask God for healing for any stuck energy in the form of emotional energy, or mental patterns that have caused limitations or anxiety. Ask for the purpose for each job, person, condition, or event in your life. Get this healing and information as you contemplate your life. Ask how it all fits together. Ask what you have learned and overcome that is helping you to become aligned with your true purpose in life.

Know that you have done good in the world. Know that your errors also have a purpose for gaining wisdom. Practice self-love and self-forgiveness. Know that you were always trying to do your best.

Know that others were also doing the best they could do at the time. Forgive and let go. It's easier from this higher perspective.

Give yourself some space. Take time to reflect and contemplate often. This is all part of transmutation and integration. While we transmute energies from the past, we are freeing energy that has served its purpose. When we do this consciously, we can then use this freed energy to give it a new purpose and use it for manifesting our true heart's desires that are in alignment with Perfection and Purpose according to our soul's blueprint and our role in God's Divine Plan.

Know your soul's powers now. Know that Source is unlimited. Know that there is an infinite amount of energy that can be transmuted, freed, and used for other purposes. Live with abundance and share it with others. Now is the time.

Self-Forgiveness

Do you ever regret any experiences that you have had? Have you ever regretted any choices you have made? Underneath that sinking feeling of regret and guilt and shame is the voice of wisdom that is ready to use the alchemical process of love to turn each experience into the gold of wisdom. Self-acceptance, acceptance of each experience as a valid lesson of love planned by our soul, and receiving God's unconditional love, are the healing aspects of love that is the process of alchemy.

Realize this deeply: "Everything works together for good for those who love God" [*Close your eyes and breathe that truth into your heart for a moment.*] Now you can sink into God's unconditional love, forgive yourself totally, completely, and permanently, and learn to love your Self, your life experiences, and God, unconditionally.

From the highest-level perspective, we are always perfect. We are Children of God—immortal beings of Light, eternally united with God. Our experiences in the human embodiment are meant to lift us from a small sense of self, to an infinite sense of Self—forever serving God's purpose.

We are never separated from God or God's unconditional love for us. The only thing that creates the illusion of separation is our perception. Perception is the key to securing our Divine conscious connection to our Source. From our small sense of self, we have a limited perception that creates the illusion of separation from God, our Source. We think that WE have to be ashamed or feel guilty and hide from God when we make perceived mistakes. We don't.

We can trust God's unconditional love and complete understanding. God's love is not human and conditional. It is not judgmental and unforgiving. Who do you think inspired Jesus to say: "Father forgive them, for they know not what they do?" Jesus demonstrated God's unconditional love for us. He demonstrated that we are eternal beings that need not fear God who is Life eternal, in which we are made in the image and likeness thereof. Nor do we need to fear anything in life including the transition of the death of our outer casing, the body...which is truly spiritual matter as we inhabit it.

Heartbreak and the Soul of Humanity

During these transitional times, we are experiencing some deep heartbreaking feelings due to the discovery of some very dark actions and harmful agendas. It's almost too hard to mention. It's pretty hard to face.

I've learned things that have happened that seemed too evil to be possible. I had the notion that humanity was an evolved race with morals, values, and goodness at its core. But to learn what has been perpetrated upon humans and animals alike, it's just hard to fathom. It breaks my heart. I cry and I pray.

This big collective heartbreak is causing a great revival. It sends us straight to God. Our faith is renewed and restored. Humility is felt deeply as we know how much we need God. We feel the pain and suffering of others. We know that people who cannot defend themselves have been targeted—the elderly and the children. Even the animals.

We have to go through the grieving process together. We need to treat each other with even more kindness and compassion. We need to heal and help others heal. We have to rebuild our society according to God's Divine Plan.

We will need to be courageous and strong. We need to be empowered to fulfill our life's missions. We have God as Source and we can develop new and better ways of being. We will rebuild and make things better than ever.

Just know that you are never alone. Give yourself time and space to heal and talk with God. This is big. The only answer is the increase in love and compassion that God sends us to receive and share with others through our hearts.

We each need to feel God's peaceful Presence. I know sometimes it feels like you got the rug pulled out from under you. It's pretty alarming when the rug gets pulled out globally and all of humanity suffers together.

This is the time you were born for. This is why you came here to help. There are no accidents. If you are receiving this message, it is meant for you personally. Take it in.

Take a deep breath and let yourself feel your feelings. Let them flow. Cry if you need to. After that you will be washed clean of old energies. God's rainbow of promises are right on the other side.

This is the rebirth. It's a rebirth of the collective consciousness of humanity. God is with us.

Get Centered and Anchored in God's Presence

We've been through a lot of initiation experiences that test our soul's resolve to align with God's will. We have been relinquishing our dependency on material possessions or specific circumstances or outcomes for our feelings. For example, have you ever been penniless, lost in the unknown, or disoriented from rapid life changes, and

THEN taken a walk in nature and just felt peace while sinking into the presence of the pure energy? Did you ever feel like nothing else mattered—that right NOW, everything feels just perfect, in Divine and perfect order, and that inner peace is here NOW?

Did you sense the Oneness, the unity, the greater love in the NOW moment? That is RESURRECTION. That is the Christ Consciousness that is emerging and transforming the flicker of the sense of our True Self into the flame that unites our soul with Spirit. The Holy Spirit is upon us revealing all Truth. It is revealing everything from inner insights, ancient wisdom, or whatever you want to call the Revelations, to seeing the truth in outer circumstances such as other's motives and "true colors" that reveal the false prophets or those without real integrity. We SEE that! That is the miracle of Christ Consciousness!

We are now here in the present moment together, as a soul family, by no accident, but by Divine Grace. Now, if you would like to partake in a Divine multi-dimensional experience that will further release the old sense of self and shed the snakeskin of old energy tied up in that false image of self, do a meditative process that will reveal even more Light of your True Christ Self. Open to perceive and receive this sublime energy of God's unconditional love, and forgive yourself. Be still, focus attention inwardly to the core of your being, and know God's love that transforms every experience into the gold of Christ wisdom. Let us acknowledge the presence of God, our angels, saints, sages, and light beings, and all God-realized beings of Light. By God's grace, we are healed.

Now take a few deep breaths and get centered in your heart, see the reflection of God's light in your single spiritual eye in your 6th chakra center at the point between your eyebrows, and perceive God's light coming in through the back of your head where it meets your spine. Now just relax and be open to receive in silence. Now open the chalice of your heart with the Love of God...do nothing but receive with deep gratitude the Golden Universal Light.

That's really all there is to it. It is a choice to open up and receive God's unconditional love, the energy that transmutes and transforms subconscious distortions of memory patterns that hold us back from expressing our full divine potential and living a life of creative freedom.

Now that love has distilled the gold of wisdom out of energy you were holding, you can express deep gratitude to glorify God. Feel appreciation for the wisdom that is interwoven into the essence of who you are, the higher purpose of life, and the transformation of being.

Hold unconditional love in your heart. Remain in a state of gratitude. Know that this is the formula for unending happiness and joy. You are perfect and perfectly loved—just as you are.

Action Steps for a Conscious Creator Lifestyle

Our inherent personal power was noted as "The Observer Effect" by scientists, but personal applications of this power are finally beginning to be realized.

The Unified Field of Consciousness is beyond duality. And yet, as humans, we deal with the dualistic nature of things. We can reconcile this paradox.

We can stay grounded in our physical dimension while accessing higher dimensions of consciousness. We can bring the new light of awareness to transform the world.

The Great Awakening and the Emergence of Higher Intelligence

During my years of studying and observing human psychology and soul development, I've seen how people can be deceived and I've seen how some rise above the attempted deception to remain or become independent thinkers. What I have come to observe and reflect on recently is the emergence of independent thinkers who have developed a higher intelligence – an intuitive ability to perceive the Truth beyond the surface.

Initially, this perception begins as cognitive dissonance. Something doesn't feel right. It feels "off" but it's not clear why. Sometimes the feeling is a strong repulsion. This cognitive dissonance leads to research. The research leads one to the Truth. Then one Truth leads to another as one goes down rabbit hole after rabbit hole of empirical evidence – the hard facts that are proven in documentation and eye-witness personal observation. Whistle blowers are the heroes of today.

Now there are large numbers of people who have evolved into a new race of humans – those of super intelligence. They have out-evolved the would-be deceptors. They out-think them at every turn.

Historically, the lower human carries the group mind of animal instinct. As the human evolves they develop their intellect. At this point one can either get stuck in the small sense of self, or move forward into the larger sense of Self. If one becomes "full of themselves" crediting all intelligence to a separate self, or ego, they become narcissistic. If they get trapped in this phase they demonstrate an intellectual ego. This intelligence is limited.

The new emerging intelligence belongs to independent thinkers; those who have moved onward and upward to a larger sense of Self; they have developed intuitive intelligence based on attunement to Truth. These people generally live in Integrity and are loving and kind. During transition, one may oscillate to some degree back and forth until true purity of consciousness is attained. There is neutrality at zero point. That's the portal where the higher mind is accessed. With a higher perspective understanding and compassion replaces judgment.

This form of intelligence marks the arrival of vibrational mastery.

Mental Evolution

To further elaborate on the mental evolution, I'll discuss the three main classes of thinking a little more.

The first are the group-minded people who tend to follow the herd blindly and obediently. They are apt to follow programs and get trapped into having to be right according to the narratives that trained them. They are limited to the instinctual mind. They are primarily carnal in nature. The second class of thinkers in human evolution has developed intellectual intelligence. The goal is to amass conceptual ideas. They don't embody these ideas; they accept them. There is a high degree of intelligence of those who gather incredible amounts of information. This development can serve either the lower self, or the higher self. The lower self tends to be a selfish self and gets stuck at this level of mental evolution. Some have become the twisted types that use their intellectual abilities to serve their carnal natures. These types are coming out in the news in our modern times. They think that they are so smart that they are above the law. They try to make the law with dark agendas and control others. However, the light of Truth has something to say to them. Just watch how this works out!

Some highly developed selfish intellectuals have become narcissistic. These types are sought after by the ones with dark agendas as they can be most used as minions to carry out their plans because they can be "bought" with big titles and big money. They can join the "club" of the elite narcissists. They are easily deceived.

When the intellect is developed and used by the higher self, it is subservient to Spirit in the realm of the soul. Spirit, or soul-realized individuals, are more selfless and have open hearts toward others. They have a higher level of tolerance, acceptance, understanding, and compassion toward others. They move on to the next level of mental evolution.

These are the third level of human intelligence. These are the intuitive independent thinkers who perceive with an open heart and open mind. They go beyond the relativities of dualistic thinking and reach the Absolute. They can discern truth from fiction without judgment or prejudice. This is the realm of the soul, or spirit. It is the field of Wholeness – the quantum holographic field of intelligence where genius is open to all.

Opening the heart and mind takes some skill. It is wise (and provides safety) to close the doors to the lower vibrational astral planes and the lower vibrations of the EMFs (electromagnetic frequencies) of the mind control technology. Energy field mastery is accomplished through shielding and assistance from higher vibrational beings that are beyond human intelligence.

The original intelligence tapped by the intuitive mind requires attunement. This is part of the vibrational mastery. It is based on Divine love of all and a realization of Oneness. This Oneness is a scientific fact as well as a resonant realization of the developed soul.

This realm of the soul is discovered and is amalgamated with the Whole of Spirit. Jesus spoke of the kingdom of the soul as the treasure, once discovered, where one would sell everything they have in order to have it.

Indeed, you can observe those who stand for truth who have lost or given up all material possessions to follow this path. Many have given their lives by dedicating themselves to finding and expressing the truth. Sacrificing one's life in service to humanity, even to the point of death, is a sign of an evolved soul. They know Infinity and they know they are Eternal. The gain is ultimately more precious and enduring than the sacrifice.

In our current evolution, we are receiving an upgrade in perception. By virtue of being attuned to Divine mind, we now perceive motives and agendas. Most of us have been fooled. However, we have experienced "cognitive dissonance" by attuning to truth. That inspired us to search farther and deeper for truth. During that process, we have developed discernment and discrimination. The "true colors" of a person becomes evident. Their secrets, lies, and ambitions come to the light of awareness. Our souls have developed, through the deepening of perception, the ability to discern the true aims and objectives, as well as the intentions and motives, of people who are not resonating with Truth. This upgrade is infiltrating the consciousness of humanity. It is the attribute of consciousness that is penetrating each soul and increases insightful intuitive abilities. This is the part of the transformation of consciousness that we are now experiencing individually, and collectively.

Cognitive dissonance is a gift from the soul. As it is developed, the conscience or Inner Light increases its ability to distinguish truth from fiction—secrets and lies are no longer accepted.

Feeling "off" leads to finding empirical evidence.

Now in our world of increased propaganda and tyrannical deceptions of global proportions, this new race of independent thinkers with intuitive perception is a power to be reckoned with. We are uniting. We are fierce.

Although this is a peaceful power; it is based in the Absolute.

In this unified peaceful power, we are seeing less and less people buying into the tactics and false information from distorted media, politicians, immoral religious "leaders", doctors, paid shills, or otherwise.

One reminder may be necessary for those seeking evolution: You can't serve money and Truth. (That doesn't mean that resources will be limited. On the contrary, abundance is coming to those who have sacrificed.) Priorities are based on love. You can't be egotistical and selfish and be humanitarian and serve humanity. In both cases, you are one or the other. In order to evolve we have to consciously choose and be dedicated and devoted to Truth and service, or money and selfish gain.

Those who are evolved control themselves. Those who are not evolved try to control others. The vast majority of the human population IS evolving into Unity Consciousness. In this New Paradigm love flows, truth reigns, peace prevails, and freedom is the platform for innovative solutions and genius creativity.

Vision Lifting

What is the consciousness activity of vision lifting? What is the purpose of vision lifting? What is the outcome of vision lifting?

The activity of vision lifting involves directing the mind away from the earthly, worldly sight of appearance and expanding the mind to the spiritual vision. The spiritual vision is a vision of perfection. The truth of God's design, of the immaculate concept of the soul, is perfection. So, when we see imperfection, we can lift our visions and create an image of perfection and present that to the universe so that the imperfect condition can be replaced by a perfect condition.

While the imperfect condition exists in lower vibrations, the energies of the heart can lift the vibration of the condition through love, understanding, and compassion. We use intention. When we pray for someone who is sick, we pray to Father God Almighty in the name of Jesus Christ to lift the person out of the condition of sickness and into the condition of wellness.

When we call on the name of Jesus Christ, we are calling on His character and His vibration—His pure soul essence---which is one with the Father. He matches the God vibration of pure love. With this vibration of pure love and the vision of perfection, we create perfection using our Divine Powers as we are unified with God in vision and vibration.

This understanding increases our abilities in being conscious creators. We do not have to buy into or accept the lower conditions. We do not have to buy into or accept the intentions, plans, or agendas of lower vibrational beings or groups. We say "No!" and we do not hold their visions or vibrations, then we stop being victims.

Steadily, we raise our vibrations and visions, and we become our True Selves operating consistently at the highest vibration. We consciously direct our thoughts to our inner knowing that reveals the blueprints of perfection. We come to know these blueprints by asking within.

Each soul has a blueprint for perfection. Mother Mary holds the vision of the immaculate conception for each soul. We can tune into

Mother Mary and ask to assist a soul by holding that immaculate conception and sending love to the individual. She did that for Jesus and helped Him on His mission. We do that with a mother's love for our children, and all the children of humanity.

No matter what the age of the physical vessel, we are all God's children (except for the serpent race who are being expelled). Attuned to God and aligned with truth and discernment, we see the Momma Bear phenomenon coming ferociously for our children right now. And you don't have to be female to get that protective energy activated! A lot of protective Papa Bears are also expressing that spirit. This is righteousness. The right use of energy.

The purpose of vision lifting is to uplift a soul to a better experience; to cause a healing or an upgrade. We can use vision lifting to create better health, to increase wealth and prosperity, to relieve anxiety, and to expel any programming that is not of the light, or of God. We can use vision lifting to raise the consciousness of humanity, to upgrade conditions of our planet—anything from government to the environment, or any other positive beneficial helpful upgrade for the betterment and well-being for the human condition.

Anything that we witness on the earthly plane that is wrong, out of balance, and of the lower vibrations can be shifted and lifted. We are compelled to use these functions of consciousness as the darkness of lower vibrational beings and activities are revealed. We are taking our power back in this way. We are rising to the occasion.

The light of our inner being is necessary in these times. As our inner light becomes increasingly activated, our outer world shifts. We are now acting through our causal nature of consciousness rather than reacting from the lower victim consciousness method which is becoming outdated. We are evolving.

The outcome of vision lifting is the essence of the intention, and better! After conceiving the higher vision and fusing it with the highest vibration of pure love, we release it to the Universe, to Great Spirit, to Father God to then amplify its benevolence. Then, we watch it manifest as Reality.

As conscious creators we are working in the field of infinite intelligence of the Oneness of All in the spirit of pure love and gratitude.

We release and give thanks. We understand the physics of consciousness as a science that is true as evidenced by the results. We have performed these conscious creations and have a storehouse of memories of perfect outcomes. What we used to call miracles are now a part of our nature as conscious creators. We know that ultimately, God the Father, the Oneness of All (that we are united with, both in will and in consciousness), is the ultimate "doer." To God the glory!

Holding the Vision for the Victory of Light

No more darkness, or shadows, or hateful scorn
Welcome the light that the morning has born
This is not just another new ordinary day
Heaven has arrived and it's here to stay

As more and more light has swept through our minds
The seekers, the warriors, and all of like kind
Have raised earth's vibrations and increased illumination
Holding the vision for a new creation

The love for God in our hearts has expanded
Bonds growing stronger as communication is candid
Pure honesty emanates truth that is known
Love is ever stronger and kindness has grown

The exposure has been hard for our hearts to endure
Because the light uncovered crimes against children so pure
We've cried within the depths of our souls to see
The pure hell of terror that evil can be

Our armies of truth and prayers to God have made
The Light of Christ to step into the shade
Our children have been rescued from tunnels underground
It's hard to fathom the level of corruption we've found

No longer deceived by narratives supporting captured agencies
Never again resting in apathetic complacency
We research the truth with intensive investigation
Lives have been saved by these truth revelations

Death has come to many who hit the truth target
Less and less buy into the lies that they market
The searchlight of truth exposes more and more crime
The fallen empire of evil has run out of time

The last scene to transition is about to unfold
It requires us to buckle up and be courageous and bold
With sovereignty, integrity, discernment, and might
We stand in solidarity to witness the Victory of Light

The Four I's of the Great Awakening

For a quick summary and to anchor in the higher consciousness just remember the four I's:

- Identity
- Intention
- Independent
- Intuitive

Identity

You are an eternal essence of divine infinite intelligence. You know your True Self identity. This is confirmation and validation that you know who you truly are. All of your inner work has paid off. Your soul is amalgamated with Spirit and you are one with Absolute Truth. You are empowered by your soul essence to step forward and live a life of mastery.

Intention

Your will power is expressed through your conscious well thought out intentions from your higher self through prayer, meditation, and deep contemplation. You set detailed conscious intentions and you create with loving attention and concentrated focus on your visions. You manifest for yourself, your loved ones, those you seek to heal or uplift or bless, your community, and for all of humanity. You focus your intentions on the success of your life's mission. You use intentions to follow your divine guidance and be the best you can be every day.

Independent

You are an independent sovereign critical thinker. You control your own mind and your life experiences. You are an awakened soul and a conscious creator. Your power of thought, feelings, words, and actions are directed entirely by you. You are successful in creating blessings for yourself and others while succeeding in your life's purpose. You are anchored in the inner strength of integrity and the power of your soul shines its light on the world and all those around you.

Intuitive

Knowing divine Oneness you are consciously connected and the highest wisdom constantly guides you and lights your path. Your perceptive abilities are awakened. You are fully activated to send and receive ideas and inspiration. You are one with the highest vibration of love and the highest vision of the pristine perfection of the divine mind. You reflect virtues and divine qualities and you give the unique gifts of your soul.

We Are Now Blessing Humanity

We are now poised to express the highest potential of our souls. We are here to give of our True Self essential nature. We receive Life.

We bear the fruit of our highest potential as we express our divinity and serve humanity, each in our own unique way, each fulfilling our personal mission that is part of God's Great Divine Plan.

Be a blessinger—a messenger of God's blessings!

Epilogue

In light of the Great Awakening and the great revival of Spirit, I can see the shifts occurring through the souls of humanity. Sometimes, I get so happy and excited that I can't sleep. Like a child at Christmas I know there are so many great things coming!

Many people I speak to tell me that they feel it, too. Although feelings oscillate because the energy shifts are so intense, overall there is a sense of positive changes on the horizon. It's like we are at this precipice and sometimes we still see the darkness, and other times we are much more in tune with the dawn.

It is my pleasure to bring the light of God through as the truth in these messages. I know this light of truth is meant specifically for these times. I feel the blessings that God is disseminating to all of His Children as He pours out His Spirit over all of us. I sense the gifts of light and love that are no less than profound.

When we gather in groups it feels like a big family reunion. We are uniting with like-minded and like-hearted people. We are magnetized by similar intentions and resonant vibrations, and we are uniting to participate in working toward creating a better world—a larger galactic experience with ultra-dimensional aspects to our conscious experiences. It really feels like love. It's a glorious time.

The massive changes in the consciousness of humanity are astounding! Although sometimes there seems to be chaos in the transition, it is clear: a re-birth is occurring. The higher consciousness of every soul is shining like a brilliant star.

Although there is still much healing and rebuilding to be done, we are equipped to make amazing positive changes. We are seizing the glimmering possibilities of certain advancements for humanity and bringing them into the world for all. What awesome gifts are here now with more coming!

With courage and strength and a renewed vitality, we are mastering the physics of consciousness, the energy of Life, as we become sovereign souls with purified spirits. Our union with God inspires the victory of Light!

As we move forward, I just know that our path is lighted by the peace from inner wisdom, love, and the grace of God. Everyone is transcending the old, and our new Heaven on Earth is being created within each one of us now. Let us step into our creation together as we live the love that we are.

The End...

...is only the Beginning when
you open your Heart!

Other Books
by Michelle Marie Angel

It IS A New World After All
Poetry and Prose to Inspire A New World Vision

Forever Free
Soul Liberation with the Holy Spirit of Truth

Bulls-Eye Faith
Believe in your True Self
Inner Work Book

www.smile4love.com

Printed in the United States
by Baker & Taylor Publisher Services